P9-CFF-387

CRAZY
ABOUT
GARDENING

CRAZY
ABOUT
GARDENING

**Reflections
on the Sweet Seductions
of a Garden**

DES KENNEDY

*Foreword
by Ann Lovejoy*

Whitecap Books
Vancouver/Toronto

Copyright © 1994 by Des Kennedy
Whitecap Books
Vancouver/Toronto

All rights reserved. No part of this publication may be reproduced,
stored in a retrieval system, or transmitted in any form or by any
means, electronic, mechanical, photocopying, recording or
otherwise, without prior written permission of the publisher.

The information in this book is true and complete to the best of
our knowledge. All recommendations are made without guarantee
on the part of the author or Whitecap Books Ltd. The author and
publisher disclaim any liability in connection with the use of this
information. For additional information please contact Whitecap
Books Ltd., 1086 West Third Street, North Vancouver, B.C.,
V7P 3J6.

Edited by Elaine Jones
Cover and interior design by Warren Clark
Cover illustration by Sylvene Trudel
Printed and bound in Canada by D.W. Friesen and Sons Ltd.,
    Altona, Manitoba

Canadian Cataloguing in Publication Data
    Kennedy, Des
        Crazy about gardening

        Includes bibliographical references.
        ISBN 1-55110-137-8

    1. Gardening—Humor. I. Title.
SB455.K45 1994   635'.0207   C93-091954-8

The publisher acknowledges the assistance of the Canada
Council and the Cultural Services Branch of the Government of
British Columbia in making this publication possible.

Contents

To Sandy —
crazy for you

Foreword

*P*hilosopher and eco-satirist, humorist and practical gardener, Des Kennedy is a unique hybrid among garden writers. Unlike most of us, his every book enriches the great library of garden writing by bringing into it something completely new. While others have offered sound advice and waxed philosophical or witty, nobody else sums up the complex whole that is garden making in quite the same way that Des does. What is it about the fellow? He is, first of all, a genuine, mad-keen gardener himself. His nails are properly grimed, and when he writes of practical gardening matters, his words have the unmistakable ring of direct and recent experience. His philosophy is equally grounded, sprouting naturally from his abiding love for the earth and the earthy. However, his range is rather wider than most, his observations supported and expanded by scholarly study, which, though cleverly disguised by humor, is nonetheless a cornerstone of his writing. Best of all, he makes us laugh at ourselves as well as each other. While relaxed and amused, we are inveigled farther afield than we might ever travel on our own. Still chuckling, we can consider unafraid truths and concepts that seem unpalatable in other contexts.

This is the truth in a nutshell: Des Kennedy makes us think hard thoughts and enjoy the exercise. Nobody else has ever made me feel that slugs could possibly live useful lives, and might even have a few, tentative charms. On the other hand, he suggests blitzing tent caterpillar nests with those handy little butane torches. Good call! Though his ecological concerns go deep, so does his fund of ridiculous stories about garden pests (some of them human). We read them and weep with laughter rather than shame, yet we are left thoughtful, prepared to make a few changes in order to improve our relationship with whatever bit of land we hold in stewardship. He manages all this because when he is coaxing us further along the garden path, it is not for our own good (always a fatal flaw in a writer), but because it is where his own heart takes him. His gift is that he can carry us along with him on his wonderful journeys.

Ann Lovejoy

Introduction

$\mathcal{D}$ocs the world really need another gardening book? Already our bookshelves bulge with volumes on every conceivable aspect of gardening. Encyclopedias sweep us from *Abelia* to *Zygopetalum*. Every week, it seems, booksellers entice us shamelessly with yet another sumptuously illustrated volume depicting gardens of impossibly exquisite beauty. A plethora of handbooks leads us step-by-common sense-step through the mechanics of composting, pruning, and propagation. It sometimes seems that there are more books about gardens and gardening than there are gardens or gardeners. Why would anybody else get involved?

"The right answer," as author and gardener Eleanor Perényi puts it, "is that a writer who gardens *is* sooner or later going to write a book about the subject." I spend most of my mornings writing, and most of my afternoons gardening. I love both occupations passionately, and so, inevitably, I've come to write a book about gardening.

Besides, writing and gardening are very similar callings. Once you've got the itch to do either, nothing this side of the apocalypse can stop you. Gardeners, like writers, are inspired by visions. They are people acclimatized to living in holy poverty, to facing horrendous adversity, all for the sake of their art. Their feelings run from heartbreak to ecstasy and back again on a regular basis. Looked at clinically, they might be diagnosed as quite mad.

I'm thinking here of people like the elderly couple I interviewed several years ago for a gardening magazine. They'd spent almost half a century creating a paradise garden out of impossible earth. Weather permitting, this pair of contented septuagenarians would spend all day outdoors amid their beloved plants. Their house was entirely overrun with rampant vines and seemed not so much neglected as almost unnecessary. I sensed they might have been as happy sleeping in a cave.

I remember being on the road back in the sixties, dropping in to an early commune located among the wild hills of New Mexico. It was a forlorn and desolate spot and most of the communards seemed given to lying around and much talking. But then I spotted the gardener in the bunch—a young guy methodically planting apple tree whips in dusty earth, lovingly firming them in with dirty hands, and watering them from a pathetic little

Mason jar. The fellow had a slightly demented look about him, an air of peevish desperation that I was too inexperienced to recognize as a classic symptom of a gardener trapped in impossible circumstances. There's a tiny garden in the middle of downtown Vancouver that glows like a small beacon of beauty through the grime of nearby parking lots, dispirited commercial buildings, and tacky nightclubs. Fashioned by a retired truck driver living in a dilapidated, turn-of-the-century wooden house, the little yard is jubilant with flowering bulbs, rose bushes, and bright annuals. Brilliantly painted miniature farm buildings, windmills, birdhouses, and flower boxes enhance the charming clutter of the yard. Doomed to disappearance, the little place is perfect where it is, its jaunty colours laughing with madcap mirth against the sombre concrete of the city, its whimsical decorations evoking fantastic images of rural simplicity while the bulldozers of urban redevelopment grind ever closer. A hand-lettered sign on the porch proclaims to passersby: "I'd rather be happy in my crazy world than to be sane and be sad."

This is the gardener precisely. A dreamer and schemer. A paradise seeker. An eternal optimist, convinced that perfection is only one rose bush move away.

Gardeners live in a landscape of the imagination where nature and culture meet. We occupy a democracy of common interests that transcends divisions of gender, class, and race, and we pay homage to the people one writer called "our green-fingered grandmothers." We work in an exhilarating alliance with nature, which is at once our muse and our nemesis, our inspiration and our undoing.

Gardeners have lessons to teach the rest of our race about how to touch the earth with affection and dexterity. About how to be happy in our crazy world. This little book celebrates the divine madness of gardeners and gardening, and that is its sole justification.

1

Gardeners

In my opinion, most gardeners are nuts. Some will deny it, of course, some will object. But the evidence is overwhelmingly against them. Just ask a person who doesn't garden, but lives with someone who does. Better yet, spend a few minutes at a flower show, a garden-club meeting, or a horticultural society soirée. These events are attended by more peculiar-looking characters than a jesters' convention in Las Vegas. The costumes are unconventional at best, the conversations quirky. The whimsical walks arm-in-arm with the eccentric, the two of them perhaps pausing to study a cluster of dead twigs in a vase. Idiosyncrasy wafts through the room like cheap perfume.

I don't say this as an outsider. I grew up in a family

wholly devoted to gardening. I fled at an early age and thought to have permanently escaped it. But years later, gardening sought me out, tracked me down like the hound of heaven and brought me back to its problematic precincts. I fell in love, not with gardening itself at first, but with a gardener and with country life, and soon all was lost. For the past two dozen years, my companion Sandy and I have lived on one of British Columbia's Gulf Islands, creating and attempting to maintain far more garden space than two people can possibly look after without suffering co-dependent nervous breakdowns. That experience, along with careful observation of other gardeners, leaves no doubt at all in my mind that gardening is a vocation of magnificent eccentricity.

Non-gardening observers sometimes speak of gardening as a hobby or pastime, as though it might be as casually taken up or dropped as playing video games or Texas line dancing. This is a dangerous misrepresentation. Gardening is a way of life, a calling. Gardeners are not dabblers. Observe them at your local nursery, listen to them on radio call-in shows and you soon realize that these are people entirely consumed. At their most extreme, gardeners become fanatics, obsessive-compulsive personalities for whom the condition of a newly purchased cryptomeria far outweighs the collapse of nation states. History itself is little more than a backdrop against which their roses might be displayed to better effect. Theirs is an all-consuming passion, an infatuation that precludes all else. "A place where the mind goes to seed," one anonymous wag described the garden.

None of this is normally discussed in public. The cognitive abnormalities seen in many gardeners have by and large failed to attract the attention of the helping professions. Diagnostic manuals seldom mention gardeners. The neurophysiological functioning of brains devoted completely to gardening is a relatively untilled field. One reason why we don't hear more about this important topic is simple enough: gardeners just don't have spare time for seeking out professional help. When there's all this seeding, thinning, and transplanting to be done, who's got time to be lying around on a Freudian couch? With spraying, staking, pruning, cutting, layering, and grafting staring you in the face, how could you possibly spare an afternoon a week for discussing your problems in a gardening recovery group? So the undeniable craziness of gardeners goes largely unnoticed by the psychotherapeutic community. Gardeners, and the families of gardeners, are left to fumble their way forward as best they might.

"Wherever a garden is an important part of family life," writes professor of landscape architecture Robert B. Riley, "we might expect it, like the house, to be an arena where intrafamily conflicts of power as well as taste are played out." We might indeed. In fact, we'd be fools not to. Various domestic configurations, from the solitude of the hermit's herb garden to the impossible entanglements of collective growing, have their pertinent quirks. I happen to live in a relationship where both my companion and I are obsessed with gardening, and our tastes more or less coincide. This type of arrangement, while not without its peculiarities, packs nowhere near the potential for fireworks of some others. For instance, two or more passionate gardeners with radically different tastes sharing one space will seldom lack for animated conversation. The divorce courts are full of such people. Even more prone to acrimony is an alignment in which an inflamed gardener attempts to ignite a matching passion in a companion who is entirely indifferent to horticulture. Generally speaking, gardeners have a somewhat limited capacity to appreciate why anyone would choose not to garden. They see it as a shortcoming, like the inability to dance, which it is their duty to help the victim overcome. In this scenario, innumerable cheap theatrics—whining, cajoling, complaining, threatening, and weeping—are commonly employed to drive the disinterested party outdoors to assist in shouldering the workload.

Arriving at the garden, whether willingly or not, companions need to develop a *modus vivendi* as to how planting decisions will be made and how chores will be allocated. In the case of a reluctant participant, who may have been browbeaten into abandoning a Sunday-afternoon football game on television, no consultation is necessary and the division of labour is straightforward: just assign a task, the more simple-minded the better. Spading, wheelbarrowing, raking, and mowing are all excellent. Weeding is not recommended, unless the weeds are sufficiently large as to be unmistakable. Grudging participants will sometimes attempt to sabotage the entire undertaking by deliberately pulling out plants they know full well not to be weeds. In such instances, horticultural counsellors recommend using positive reinforcement while gently moving the destructive worker to a simpler task. Under no circumstances should miscreants be banished from the garden, as this is precisely what they want.

When two or more participants have an equal investment in a garden, as in my own case, tactical sagacity is of utmost importance. Step one, I think, is to stake your turf. In a somewhat traditional motif, I've assumed a loose primacy in the vegetable patch and orchard while Sandy more or less reigns over most things ornamental. In my domain, strutting about like Mussolini among the zucchinis, I suffer scant interference. Other people are scarcely allowed through the gate, and never encouraged to touch anything. I recognize my attitude is aberrant, brought on partly by a brief but disillusioning fling with communal gardening in our early "back to the land" days. I find the concept of communal gardening attractive enough in the abstract, and I admire examples of where it has worked—in established communes, religious groups, and among inner-city dwellers reclaiming their neighbourhoods through collective gardening projects. But my own experience of sharing garden space with others has left a distinctly sour aftertaste. A solitary soul by nature, for me communal gardening is, like group sex, something best experimented with in youth and then set forever aside.

A second line of defence in companionable planting is to assume an expertise in the chores you enjoy doing and feign absolute incompetence in the ones you don't. Take bulb planting, for example. There are few aspects of gardening I dislike more than planting bulbs. There's the tedium of trying to place them so that their browning foliage won't be an eyesore after blooming; potential colour clashes are a perpetual problem; there are precise planting depths to keep straight for each genus; and there's an unwritten rule decreeing that wherever you dig into earth in order to plant a bulb, you'll invariably slice through at least two established bulbs you'd forgotten were there. Of course, you don't want to be without them—what would spring be without windy daffodils or the magical chalices of tulips? No, the secret of success is to manoeuvre one's companion into doing the dirty work of planting them. At all costs, look busy. Elaborate displays of huffing and puffing—random wheelbarrowing of compost, rolling of stones, and similar diversions—can work wonders here. If all else fails, fire up a machine of some sort—chain saws, leaf shredders, and lawnmowers are all effective around bulb-planting time. The point is: look too busy for bulbs.

It goes without saying that one must be constantly alert against countermeasures by a companion. Not long ago Sandy decided to uproot several thousand old daylilies and replant them in a wild corner of the garden. In this, she said, she "needed help"—a phrase that, experience has taught me, is code for "I would like you to do this." I dislike breaking up and replanting daylilies almost as thoroughly as I do planting bulbs. I responded to her request with a really quite brilliant array of diversionary tactics. Sandy parried with a master stroke, producing several large bagfuls of bulbs to be planted. A stalemate ensued as we each worked with exaggerated diligence at our separate tasks while the confounded daylilies sat in an accusatory pile. Eventually, with the ground near freezing and the roots near dead, I caved in and planted the wretched things. But the following spring, there was a last laugh to be laughed as we discovered that I'd inadvertently (of course) planted most of the roots crown-downwards. Touché!

The tactical give-and-take required within a family unit is, however, mere child's play compared to dealing with the neighbours. "Love your neighbour, yet pull not down your hedge," admonishes an old adage. If there is one fundamental problem with neighbours, it is their stubborn refusal to acknowledge that your premises represent a landscaping ideal towards which they too ought to aspire. Some sin by omission, neglecting their places so that they become unkempt and derelict looking. A later chapter, dealing with lawn maintenance, examines the awesome neighbourhood power that can be mobilized against such sluggards. Less easily brought to heel, but no less infuriating, are gardening overachievers. You know the type: not a weed to be seen anywhere, not a blade of grass out of place, trees and shrubs selected tastefully and pruned to perfect proportion, hedges meticulously sheared, impeccable floral displays for every season. And always so damnably jolly. These artistes are invariably a step ahead of the latest trend—they'd already become "power gardeners" while the rest of us were still trying to figure out if pink flamingoes on the lawn were high kitsch or hopelessly passé. But their perfectionism grates where it aims to impress. They go too far.

The most virulent of this type eventually descend into an unseemly snobbery. A garden snob is a snob of the very worst sort. The vanity of the art gallery is nothing, the snootiness of the recital hall a small foible in comparison with the hauteur of a true-bred garden snob. Your cleverest planting schemes can quickly wilt beneath the gaze of such a visitor. What had seemed to be an arrangement of uncommon charm and beauty dwindles into something ordinary, something really quite commonplace, something almost vulgar.

Dread of vulgarity haunts the gardener's emotional life, and it is this dread that the sophisticate exploits. The ingenuous gardener is subtly manipulated into suspecting that there exists somewhere a listing of admissible plants, a catalogue of acceptable colours which she or he has never seen. The snob has. The snob just about wrote the catalogue, or at least translated it from the original Greek. "Oh, look: portulacas! How brave you are!" smiles your visitor, and you know instantly that portulacas are simply "not done." Or cannas. Or yuccas. Looking around forlornly, you realize that almost everything in your garden is "not done."

And your choice of colours! How could you have entertained so many brassy reds, such shockingly gaudy yellows? Too late you realize that you should have planted for demure white and tasteful cool blue blossoms, always with restraint, emphasizing the textures of foliage and its various hues of green. What were you possibly thinking of with that outlandish splash of variegated nasturtiums? As for your red-hot pokers, the less said the better.

A harmless subspecies of the preening peacock are those blinkered souls who can see no garden save their own. Encountering a magnificent display of blossoming antique roses in some other garden, they'll tell you at great length about the rose bushes they're planning to order next autumn. Any plant is noteworthy only in its relationship to their own efforts: Gee, my cabbages are well ahead of those; I wonder how these azaleas would fit in at my place; Oh, I much prefer the white lilies I grew this year to these! A tour through any garden, public or private, magnificent or mean, becomes in the company of these persons an arms-length tour of their gardens instead.

Most gardeners, it goes without saying, are not at all given to self-absorption, much less to supercilious snobbery; quite the reverse. You pop in for a visit and you'd think they'd been caught naked in the most compromising of positions. "Oh! there's nothing in bloom just now," they'll blurt out, "the place is an absolute shambles; I haven't had a minute to spare out there; what a terrible year it's been for weeds." Their gardens will look perfectly lovely to everyone but them. "Oh, you should have been here last week!" they'll exclaim, no matter what week you show up. These people live in the strange state of always having had a better garden a week ago, of always being, like unemployed actors, "between shows."

Most gardeners are grand talkers, and many are given to shameless name-dropping. But there's one special breed of gardener that stands head and shoulders above the rest when it comes to garden talk. A conversation among these people is so peppered with strange, polysyllabic volleys you'd think you were hearing a congregation of evangelicals talking in tongues. These characters occupy the horticultural highlands of botanical nomenclature, an elevated region in which the highest good is the precise identification of any plant by its complete formal name.

Botanical nomenclature bestows upon those who wield it well a prestigious authority. If you can distinguish a *Delphinium cheilanthum formosum* 'Belladonna' from a 'Bellamosum' of the same variety, you've got some real bargaining chips. I cannot and do not, and I'll tell you why: in a former incarnation I spent eight years as a seminarian, then a novice, and finally a monk in a strict Roman Catholic monastic order. When the monastery bell tolled at two in the morning and we stumbled sleepily out of bed and down to chapel to chant the solemn verses of matins and lauds, our antiphonal chanting was in Latin. We ate and drank Latin. Perversely, we told old Latin jokes. The very air we breathed seemed suffused with musty Latin. As a consequence, I have a highly developed aversion to the stuff. But it puts one at considerable disadvantage in a volley of botanical oneupmanship. Calling something a "ghostplant," for example, simply doesn't resonate with the solemn authority of *Graptopetalum paraguayense*.

Linnaeus, the mad genius who revolutionized and standardized the naming of plants about 250 years ago, should be honoured as every gardener's faithful companion. Before he got to work categorizing plants by genus, species, subspecies, and variety, descriptive Latin names sometimes ran on for several lines.

Unfortunately, not every gardener adheres strictly to the Linnaean system. Despite the great Swedish naturalist's best efforts, and various compelling reasons for mastering botanical lingo, some of us are fully determined to not get the names right. Perfectionists, of course, tag their plants properly and keep meticulous records as to what varieties are what. The rest of us prefer to lose the nursery name tags—half of which aren't correct to begin with—and not quite get around to writing down the names while still fresh in mind. The memory no longer being quite what it once was, gaps develop. Even the familiar common names begin to slip after a bit. Sandy and I often engage in long absurdist exchanges in which we're both trying mightily to identify a familiar plant by name. Guttural vowel sounds and gestures predominate, as in those clumsy conversations you attempt with people with whom you don't share a language.

Those gardeners who are not prevaricators by nature, when caught out not knowing a plant's proper name, often trot out the old standby, "It was given to me by somebody who didn't know what it was." This suffices when talking to triflers, but serious plantspeople are apt to respond, as one did to me recently, with, "It would be worthwhile researching it." Our old friend and fellow islander Hamish is a far more artful dodger. Long married to a superb gardener and nomenclatural wonderworker in her own right, Hamish has developed a sly routine for whenever he's stuck for a plant's identity. He boldly fabricates false Latinisms. If asked by some unsuspecting visitor what a certain plant is, Hamish will glance at it and drolly announce something like, "Oh, that's a *pseudocatapultus* actually." This sort of shameless deception is not generally recommended.

A more wholesome strategy, and one many gardeners adopt, is to stick with the old nicknames that plants have picked up over the years. I like these vernacular names because they connect us with generations of gardeners who have gone before us. The common names by which they knew plants may be altogether lacking in precision, but they more than compensate for that with charm. I think more fondly of the scarlet pimpernel by its peasant names—"shepherd's warning" and "poor man's weather glass" from the plant's habit of closing its tiny yellow blossoms at the approach of a storm—than by its proper credentials, *Anagallis arvensis*. As American garden writer Louise Beebe Wilder pointed out long ago, the old nicknames—the cowslip called "jackanapes on horse-back," the footloose "roaming Charlie" or the periwin-kle called "sorcerer's violet"—sustain a bond between gardeners of today and those of past generations. "They reach us across the years like messages from old friends," wrote Wilder, and hold a secret power "to spread a magic carpet for the mind and send it voyaging into gardens of the past."

From these past gardens, too, we inherit a cast of colourful-sounding characters who live on in our gardens through the plants that bear their names. I like these people on principle: dutiful Mrs. Bradshaw, effervescent Lady Betty Balfour, even dour-sounding Frau Karl Druschki. But, to avoid disillusionment, I've learned it's wise not to inquire too thoroughly into their back-grounds. Take the unmasking of Miss Willmott as a case in point. I knew nothing about this woman other than that several flowers bear her name. One that we have in our garden is a delightful perennial, a dwarf potentilla with magenta-rose flowers commonly called Miss Willmott. The name encouraged us to personalize the plant and say foolish things such as, "Miss Willmott seems to have enjoyed her summer shower today."

This charming plant appeared so good-hearted, gen-tle, and unassuming that we somehow supposed its namesake had been the same. I pictured her as a dear old soul who puttered in her cottage garden, freely gave away surplus produce to the neighbours, and was beloved by all for miles about. But eventually I discovered that Ellen

Willmott, one of the great gardeners and plant collectors of the late nineteenth century, was neither gentle nor good-hearted. Her biographer described her as "absolutely infuriating and quite impossible to deal with." Her grand garden at Varley Place was staffed by a crew of gardeners whom she compelled to work in ostentatious outfits of navy blue aprons, green silk ties, and green straw boaters. If they had to cross a roadway on the estate, the workers removed and folded their aprons, carried them across and then put them back on again. Rather than the charming cottage gardener her named flowers evoke, Willmott seems to have been an autocratic crackpot and full-blown garden snob to boot.

Most gardeners are mad for exchanging plants with one another. Drop in for a quick visit and they'll pile you up with flats and boxes bulging with new seedlings, slips, and scions. Particular care should be taken to avoid these types at perennial-dividing time. "Oh, I just couldn't bear to throw them out!" they'll exclaim, while heaping you up with huge clumps of Siberian iris roots. One acquaintance of ours insists on bestowing upon us bags of fiercely orange tiger lily bulbs every autumn. What can you say?

Of course there are advantages to this underground economy among plantspeople. Among the plants that I like best are those originally given to us by friends, because they possess an extra dimension, combining their own beauty with one's feelings for the people who made a gift of them. The garden becomes a vivid scrap-book full of living mementos of friends and all-but-forgotten passersthrough. One of our favourite herbaceous peonies is an early-blooming species given to us by Dora Drinkwater, an old-time islander who lives in a charming clapboard house down by the general store. Our little island's answer to Miss Marple, Dora can be seen helping out at the community library or sipping her coffee at the local café. But we also see her with perfect clarity every spring when the luminescent amber stalks of her peony emerge from the earth. In the warm days of May the plant produces multiple flower buds like tiny green globes all delicately veined. An infinitesimally thin red line bisects each bud; then as the bud swells, the green veins grow deeper and the bisecting red line widens and seems almost to bleed into the green. At last splitting open, the bud reveals a tiny frill of red petal, like the glimpsed hem of a demure petticoat. In the sun's warmth, the emerging cluster of petals elongates and their green cap falls back, freeing the petals to unfold voluptuously until their rich red double blooms form a sumptuous half globe of velvet flowerage. For us, Dora is inseparable from this extraordinary unfolding.

My dad's another and different case in point. His garden, just above the Humber River in Toronto, boasts all kinds of beautiful but unpretentious plantings, none more spectacular than his beloved perennial hibiscus. A southern plant aptly named great rosemallow, *Hibiscus moscheutos* towers well over two metres high with a plenitude of huge pale pink or red blooms. At least at his place it does. Years ago he sent us some cuttings, but under our care they fall far short of the splendid show of blooms he achieves each July. We're lucky to coax out half a dozen reluctant flowers by September. Maybe we don't water them enough; maybe our summers are just a bit too cool for them; or maybe—what son can avoid this suspicion?—I'm just not as good a gardener as he is. If the plants had come from some indifferent nursery, we'd have given them the heave-ho long ago. But, coming from where they do, they carry considerable baggage, and year after year I labour mightily to see if I can't get them up to snuff.

Speaking of getting things up to snuff, there is no event guaranteed to get a garden shipshape more surely than having it showcased as part of a garden tour open to the public. Even the most reclusive of gardeners is hard-pressed to resist an opportunity to have their handiwork acknowledged by crowds of admirers. A tour of private gardens serves to attract a great many eccentric characters to a location normally occupied by only a few. Whimsicality is compounded through curiosity.

Several years ago our local land conservancy was strapped for funds to purchase some forest land containing rare old trees being menaced by a logger-developer. Illuminated by the particular genius that hovers around desperation, Sandy conceived the idea of a Country Cottage and Garden Tour. For twelve dollars a head, we calculated, we could shepherd a few hundred visitors around local estates and, in the words of the folksy capitalist hoax, find ourselves "laughing all the way to the bank." Brilliant!

We set about determining which properties to feature. Simple though it might seem, this process quickly evolved into the emotional equivalent of attending a long-postponed family reunion at which, despite everyone's best intentions, serious dysfunctions begin to manifest. Judgements must be made. Irving and Mary-Lou's dahlia patch is quaint enough in its own way, but wouldn't Melody's herb garden be more intriguing? Dare we ask the Browns? Dare we not ask the Heinemanns?

The home-owners eventually chosen soon became possessed by a frenzied perfectionism. Tasks that had sat unfinished for decades were miraculously completed. Secateurs flashed in the springtime sun like the swords of samurai. Weeds leapt from the earth in terror. Lawnmowers roared. Island unemployment rates plummeted as extra help was hired.

One question hung like rampant honeysuckle above the enterprise: would anybody come? Three weeks before the event, we'd scarcely sold a ticket. The organizing committee masked its misgivings behind a façade of bullishness that would do a penny stock promoter proud. All would be well. And so it was. Tickets soon sold out; success was at hand. But wait! Is that a cloud on the horizon? Yes. In fact, as the fateful weekend crept closer there was no horizon at all, only a solid leaden sky menacing with the threat of rain.

Saturday dawned wet and dreary. Our worst nightmare. Who in their right minds would venture out in this miserable drizzle? We sat commiserating over coffee at about 8 A.M., two hours before the tour was to begin. Looking up, we saw a troop of strangers march ebulliently into the yard and commence a cheery conversation. "Hope you don't mind if we're a few minutes early!" chirped one. Seeing these rain-soaked earlybirds gave the first of many indications that, in our preparatory anxieties, we had failed to factor in one vital component: the mad fanaticism of garden fanciers.

They came in hordes after that. Droves of them. Multitudes of them. About eight hundred people tromped determinedly through our gardens and home over the two days. Many had questions. And supplementary questions. What's that blue flower over by the wall? I say, this little tree isn't a *Daphniphyllum macropodum* is it? We have scores of plant species in the garden. On a very good day I can remember the names of about six of them. After eight hours of mind-numbing questioning by hundreds of inquisitive spectators, I couldn't tell a hosta from a hose pipe.

Inescapably, there had to be a know-it-all or two in the crowd. "What's that lovely rose?" somebody asked me. Desperately I searched the abandoned caverns of my brain for an answer. Nothing. "It's a 'Madame Isaac Perriere', " sniffed another visitor, her tone plainly implying that if I didn't know what it was I had no right trying to grow it. By the end of the second day we were virtually brain-dead. I could only watch with slack-jawed bemusement as a horde of little boys ran up and down the rock garden—a misdemeanor that would normally provoke an elephantine shriek of outrage.

Of course, I exaggerate. In truth, the visitors were absolutely exemplary and undeniably delightful. Gardening people at their finest. Not a thing went missing; not a plant was damaged. Despite the gloomy weather a spirit of convivial celebration suffused the whole weekend, and our conservancy coffers bulged with profits. Naturally, the event has now become an annual ritual, offering a useful way for even the gardening recluses among us to share our private spaces with a great many appreciative people.

A garden tour, like other gatherings of gardeners, provides a grand opportunity to re-experience the magnificent eccentricities of the gardening public. The hushed tones in which some speak. The clasped notebooks or scraps of paper upon which inscrutable messages are scrawled. The prodigious capacity for stooping, sniffing, and exclaiming. Is it my imagination, or do all the men bear an uncanny resemblance to Capability Brown? Don't most of the women remind you somehow of Gertrude Jeckyll? Even more disconcerting, have you noticed the tendency among gardeners who specialize in certain species, a tendency to resemble their plants, the way pet owners begin looking like their pets? Alpine gardeners gradually shrinking into wizened little characters with brilliant smiles and tiny, glittering eyes. Iris fanciers who, even while wearing the most sensible of outfits, seem to be walking in elegant procession down the central aisle of Westminster Abbey. Do all gladiolus growers wear Hawaiian shirts and drink too much?

These remarkable metamorphoses, I believe, bear witness to the enchantments plants can cast across our lives. Gardeners, after all, are dabblers in magic, comrades with wizards and witches, magicians and alchemists. They are shrouded in mysteries, poring over their cabalistic catalogues, puzzling out the riddles of rhizomes, deciphering the runes on rutabagas. Their ways are as inscrutable as the arcane twistings of wisteria, as enigmatic as hens and chicks.

Gardeners commune with spirits. Under the sweet enchantment of plants, exhilarated by idyllic summer afternoons spent in the dappled shade of sacred groves, the gardener wanders off into strange realms where elves and dryads dance in moonlit clearings and the little people play. Nymphs and sylphs seem to flit among the bluebells; faeries sip silver drops of dew from the lips of lady's mantle. The spirits of friends long dead or far away or half-forgotten begin humming old folk tunes behind the hollyhocks. And all is well in the garden, all is well.

2

Time

 $\mathscr{E}$very so often one runs across a magazine or newspaper article that breathlessly discloses that gardening is now North America's favourite hobby. The report will burble on about the phenomenal new interest in gardening and cite recent studies that show gardening has now eclipsed bowling as the nation's most popular pastime. I have no quarrel with these reports, other than their tone of Moses-on-the-mountain revelation.

As often as not, the same publication, or one right next to it on the newsstand, will carry an equally razzmatazz account of how nobody has any true leisure time any more. I saw one of these articles recently, citing data from Statistics Canada that the average work week (for those fortunate enough to have a job) has declined from

41.5 hours in 1966 to 36.8 hours in 1992, leaving a lot of people with considerably more free time on their hands. But here's the supposed shocker: people now enjoy less, not more, leisure time than previously. Nobody gets to loll around in a hammock anymore. No one's got time to read a book for the pure simple pleasure of it. How can this be? What's going on? Authorities in recreation and leisure pursuits show remarkable imagination in concocting hypotheses as to why extra free time isn't resulting in more leisure. Astonishingly, the experts overlook the obvious: a growth in the popularity of gardening on the one hand, evaporation of leisure time on the other. You don't need a doctorate in the demographics of leisure to know what's going on; all you need is a garden.

"All the clocks were thrown out of heaven," Saul Bellow wrote, and I remember vividly the day that I cast my own watch aside. It was shortly after arriving at our new island home, a time when we were just beginning to flirt with serious gardening. For years I'd been one of those compulsive types who needs to look at a watch every few minutes for background reassurance. But, having gone "back to the land," I no longer needed to know what time of day it was, or even what day of the week it was. With no meetings to go to or appointments to keep (ah, blessed freedom!), hours and days were all pretty much of a piece. It was either early or late, I was either hungry or not. Boldly I stripped off my old Timex, stuck it in a drawer somewhere, and never put it on again.

We were faced in those days with enough strenuous work to give the pyramid-builders pause. There was land to be cleared, earth to be broken, a home to be built—all with few available resources save muscle power and the immortal energy of youth. Yet somehow we also made time for summer baseball games on Sunday afternoon, for long hours drifting on the lake fishing for trout for supper. There was enough spare time to ramble through the June woods picking sweet wild huckleberries for a pie. Our pace in those halcyon days had something of the cyclic good sense of the hunter-gatherer. All this, as I say, was a prelude to becoming serious gardeners.

Nowadays when I hurry down to our little general store to mail some letters or pick up a parcel, there'll often be small clusters of young people hanging around outside, smoking cigarettes, lying with their oversized dogs on the lawn of the little Anglican church or playing with juggling sticks. Some of these kids are locals, others are itinerants sometimes known as "shrubbies" either from their hairy appearance or from their habit of sleeping in the bush when no better accommodation offers itself. They're plainly poor, some of them homeless, but they're enviably rich in the leisurely time of youth. None of them, so far as I know, has a garden.

Dashing back home to get the squash seedlings transplanted out while there's still a bit of cloud cover, I've scarcely got time to reflect on the cruel hoax being played here. It is this: that behind the incessant activity, deep in the very heart of gardening, pulses an attempt to remember and recapture the sweet freedom, the blessed dis-imprisonment of childhood. "Much of gardening is a return," writes author Michael Pollan in *Second Nature*, "an effort at recovering remembered landscapes." Or half-remembered landscapes, dreamscapes, or enchanted sanctuaries imprinted on our tribal unconscious. This helps explain why so many gardeners are given to standing around in melancholy Byronic poses, united with the great romantics in longing for a simpler time, a cleaner, safer and less crowded world where nature exults in all her rich beneficence.

After a few glasses of chilled wine under the rose arbour, the reminiscent gardener begins to bask in the ambience of antiquity which suffuses every fine garden. Here time and timelessness play against one another, like dappled sunlight and shadows on a wall. Seasons and years tangle together as inextricably as the tendrils of a rampant clematis, past and future knotting in a cyclic wholeness. It's been said that a garden is the one place on earth where history does not assert itself; perhaps not, but it certainly insinuates itself in cunning ways. You can't gaze into a *Rosa mundi* rose without experiencing a romantic thrill born somewhere in the hills of ancient Persia. Within the antique bloom's pink and white beauty you can almost hear the prophet Mohammed promising the pious "a blissful abode / Gardens and vineyards / Damsels with swelling breasts of suitable age / And a brimming cup."

The great religions teach that we began in a garden, whether it was called Eden or by some other name. The fundamental charm of the best-made gardens is that they lift us out of time, transport us subconsciously into the timelessness of our ancestors, to the mythical garden in which we feel perfectly at home, profoundly at peace. Touched by remembrances of things past, by intimations of immortality, the gardener succumbs to a nostalgia both sweet and sad. Weary of an imperfect world, one's spirit longs to return to that primordial state of innocent bliss. What was it old Wordsworth wrote?

...But there's a Tree, of many, one,
A single Field which I have looked upon,
Both of them speak of something that is gone:
     The Pansy at my feet
     Doth the same tale repeat:
Whither is fled the visionary gleam?
Where is it now, the glory and the dream?

It's probably out in the potting shed trying to remember where it left the green twine. Nostalgia, as one wag put it, is a seductive liar. Romantic longings for the lost innocence of childhood or the myths of Avalon won't get any potatoes planted. Conscious of already having sat for too long, the gardener lurches up and staggers back out to work. Grounded in the here and now, there's no escaping the immutable natural law which dictates that, no matter how large or small a garden might be, there is never enough time to complete the work it requires. There are always more jobs to be done than can be done in the allotted time. Similarly, at any given moment in the gardening cycle, the scores of chores needing to be done will all appear to be of equal importance.

Let me give you a specific case. It is a stunningly beautiful morning in the last week of May as I write this. Here is an abbreviated list of the chores that absolutely *must* be done this afternoon. I have eight adolescent zucchini plants, raised from seed and now bursting their small pots, that should have been transplanted out a week ago. (Why anybody of sound mind would cultivate eight zucchini plants is not a question I'm prepared to entertain until August.) Alongside the zucchini squat several dozen pepper plants and about a dozen eggplants also demanding relocation. Corn, carrots, parsnips, and beans should all have been planted by now but haven't been. The lawns have remained uncut for so long their lush spring growth may have to be scythed before the lawnmower can get through. Lanky comfrey and stinging nettle plants surrounding the vegetable patch are setting seeds, as are the ferny mounds of sweet Cicely in the rhododendron garden. Unless cut to the ground this afternoon, all three will produce several million invasive seedlings. Ditto for innumerable dandelions. All the fruit trees need tip pruning right away. Yesterday I noticed armies of ants marching purposefully up the trunks of several apple trees, and clusters of aphids on the new spring growth. The aphids need spraying with insecticidal soap and the tree trunks should get a band of Tanglefoot paste to keep the ants off. Up along the fence line there's another colony of ants whose workers are methodically chewing off the newly-opening flower buds of one of our favourite roses. All the summer-flowering clematis need tying up if they're not to become the same hopeless tangle they were last year. A number of the peonies are suffering botrytis blight; the affected leaves should be picked off and burned without delay. Four or five of the roses seem to have fire blight, and their afflicted canes should also be removed and burned. All the vegetables and annuals that we planted in the last several weeks need watering, weeding, and mulching. Two large clumps of alstroemeria have issued an ultimatum that if they're not staked immediately, they'll fall flat on their fannies by tomorrow. And there are about twenty kilograms of rhubarb to be harvested and processed for wine.

The list goes on and on, off into infinity. Every gardener I know has a compilation to match or surpass this one. In our marvellous diversity, we respond in different ways to the crises of the moment. The indecisive among us spend an inordinate amount of time trying to decide in what order to do the chores and which to do first. As a consequence, nothing much gets done at all and twilight soon descends. You often see these types standing in their gardens staring blankly out into space and muttering to themselves.

At the opposite extreme we find gardeners who practise what trend watchers now call "time deepening." This is the supposed art of doing a number of different activities simultaneously. It's a trick long known to mothers everywhere, but now given a fancy new name as a byproduct of the cellular-phone and laptop-computer approach to life. Time deepening may work passably in a brokerage house, but in the garden it's a strategy that can only have a tragic end. Practitioners can be recognized by twitches, tics, and uncontrollable shaking. Their gardens are generally littered with weed heaps, implements, and half-transplanted flats of near-dead seedlings. These people specialize in leaving their rakes lying flat on pathways, then stepping on the tines and having the handle fly up and smack them in the face. As often as not they don't notice.

Some gardeners—a distinct minority, almost a rare and endangered subspecies—have refined their time management techniques so as to eliminate all hurly-burly from the undertaking. These are invariably people whom it is difficult to like. "We list and prioritize," they'll inform you, with an unmistakable whiff of smugness. "No use driving yourself crazy dashing from one thing to another, doing none of them very well and not enjoying any of them." These platitudes are usually delivered at a time when you're doing precisely that. "I'm into time deepening," you'll reply. That gets them started on how they develop their gardening agendas by listing and prioritizing. "We simply write down everything we need to do, then we rank them in order of 'must do.' Of course, we always ask ourselves: how many of these chores can we realistically and enjoyably accomplish today? Then we get started." By this point you're tempted to accidentally splash their perfectly pressed summer whites with some of the manure tea you're bucketing over to the potted geraniums. Oblivious, they carry on: "We like to do each task thoroughly and well, enjoying the doing, and stop when it's time to stop. We find this method eliminates chaos and confusion, and allows you to proceed with tranquility and the reassuring sense of things being surprisingly well in hand."

Of course you're too polite to say so, but most of us would rather not waste precious time sitting around listing and prioritizing. It smacks of those human-growth workshops in which participants have to articulate their hopes and fears. We prefer grumbling. Gardeners may be the greatest grumblers in the world, and scarcity of time—along with the vicissitudes of the weather—is a favourite theme. "There just aren't enough hours in the day," we like to complain, as though we're being deliberately short-changed of hours by some unscrupulous timekeeper. Ecclesiastes might ramble on about there being "a time to plant, and a time to pluck up that which is planted," but we don't think so. We know there's never enough time for either. And it's hard to tell whether the planting or the plucking up is worse.

At our place, by about halfway through September, we find ourselves trapped beneath an avalanche of garden produce. Tomatoes are among the worst. We grow about half a dozen varieties, maybe fifty plants in all. When the fruits are in full flow, it's a full-time job just keeping up. We freeze some and dry some and simmer some down to tomato sauce and hot sauce for freezing— and still there are scores more, ripening on newspapers spread all over the kitchen floor. Huge armloads of Swiss chard and beetroots, celery and sweet corn get trundled into the house to be set by for winter. And zucchini, of course, infestations of zucchini, plagues of them. By early October avid gardeners can be found wandering the byways trying to give away surplus squash and other produce. Even local food-bank workers cringe when these over-productive gardeners arrive bearing boxes overflowing with wilted greens. Objects of considerable pity, nobody has the heart to tell these zealous gardeners that they're victims of their own foolish miscalculations. There's precious little sympathy for those who, year after year, grow far more produce than they can possibly deal with, all the while complaining that the garden takes up so much of their time.

Under such a regime, it really is important for gardeners to do away with any idle thoughts about enjoying other pursuits. You may long to go tramping through the cloud rainforests of Costa Rica or take up ocean kayaking, but be reasonable: will the garden let you? Unless they can slip away in the dead of winter, gardeners' vacations generally end up being truncated little outings like the furtive one-nighters of philanderers. And the whole time they're away they're worrying about the greenhouse temperature or fretting about the trespasses of neighbourhood dogs. The only form of extended vacation that's really acceptable is to go on a tour of fine gardens elsewhere. Experiencing the gardens of great manicured estates provokes a profound sense of the inadequacy of one's own small efforts and a burning desire to rush home and get to work on a whole new landscape scheme. Generally speaking, gardeners, like oysters, are better off not going anywhere.

Timing is everything. If we can't escape and can't prioritize, we tell ourselves, we should at least attempt to set a civilized tempo to the working. We deserve the opportunity to pause, to look about and bask in the sweet delights of the garden. For precisely these moments of aesthetic interlude, Sandy and I have created a number of resting places throughout our gardens, benches located at strategic points from which particularly pleasing aspects of the place can be savoured. We never quite get around to actually sitting in these lounging areas, but happily the benches do double duty as assembly points for tools, flats, empty pots, discarded clothing, and the like. Which is also why a rough, hand-built bench is just as serviceable as those elegant English benches of curved teak that you see in the coffee-table books.

Gardeners can suffer from a chronic inability to be in the present moment. That's because, like Joan of Arc, we're afflicted with future visions. I'll give you an example: on the wall just outside our front door grows a magnificent spring-blooming clematis. Now about eight years old, and finally reaching the full glory of maturity, it pours down a three-metre cascade of deep blue flowers of exquisite delicacy. If we stop for a moment to contemplate the plant, we're almost bowled over by its beauty. But here's the rub: several years ago we planted two more clematis at other spots along the house front. Still getting themselves settled, in the excruciatingly slow manner of clematis, these vines now each produce only a couple of flowers—but what gorgeous flowers! hearts of gold, petals of velvety maroon suffused with black silk. All three vines bloom simultaneously and play against one another brilliantly. As stunning as the older, blue-flowering vine appears, I now can't look at it without visualizing the future scene when all three plants are mature and flowering profusely together. How divine it will be! The impatient part of me wants to fast-forward about five years just to behold the transcendent beauty of that scene. That's how a real and present delight is bartered for an imaginary future.

Every new plant brought in, every new planting scheme dreamed up, is with an eye to future effect. You recognize that there's a cunning interplay of pastel pinks involving pink-flowering lupins, salmon-pink oriental poppies and some recently acquired Exbury hybrid azaleas. But there's a bit of a blank spot....It could use something else.... Suddenly inspired, you make a mental note: next fall, you'll lift those lovely white- and pink-flowering irises from the back garden, and put them in here. Then, just think how grand the setting will look! You can almost see it now: next year's garden, a thing of unqualified beauty, blooming perpetually in the gardener's fertile imagination. Never included in the vision are the necessary changes next year's compositions will invariably demand. The imaginary garden is always perfect, whereas the real garden, evolving through time, is constantly approaching—although never quite attaining—perfection. It resembles that old brain-teaser in physics whereby you can never arrive at a given point because of the infinite number of times that you can halve the distance between yourself and the point. No matter how gorgeous a garden is, no matter how enthusiastically visitors extol its glory, the gardener still fusses about with an eye towards improvement, correcting mistakes, refining the vision, inching a little closer to perfection.

One thing's certain: in the garden, nothing's static. Even if you were to achieve a triumph of garden design one year, a horticultural tour de force in which all shapes, colours, forms, textures fit together impeccably, you couldn't hold it there for long. Trees and shrubs that are perfectly proportioned and properly spaced at ten years old may be elbowing one another rudely in another decade's time. A few more years and you're having to decide which of several precious trees will have to be felled (oh, woe!) for the good of the others. The garden designed for today is of necessity very different from the one that will work tomorrow.

And, of course, most certain of all is death. If it weren't for death in the garden, the body of world literature would be considerably more slender than it is. Horticultural dyings-away have provided a reliable bread-and-butter theme long before and long since Elizabethan poet Robert Herrick penned his immortal lines:

Gather ye Rose-buds while ye may,
Old Time is still aflying:
And that same flower that smiles today,
Tomorrow will be dying.

A regular browser at literary rummage sales, Will Shakespeare picks up the same theme and gives it a different spin with a military metaphor:

O, how shall summer's honey breath hold out
Against the wrackful siege of battering days?

How indeed. Mortality stalks the garden like one of the Bard's convenient ghosts. Things are barely getting under way in early spring when the snowdrops falter and fall away. Even though the full glory of the summer garden still awaits, the sad collapse of tulips strikes a melancholy note. Sharing the poet's sensibility, the gardener experiences a small tremor of grief at their passing. They've given such moments of rapture, and now they're gone, seemingly before their time. Cruelly, the tragedy recurs throughout the growing season. "Oh, don't tell me the fraxinella are finished already!" Once again we stand aghast at the predictable.

More stubborn than smart, some part of us rebels against this dying-away, stiffens against the decay. We long to hold the garden at its apex, let it flaunt its full-blown beauty as though it were immortal. And we can't, blast it all, we can't! It slips away and soon is gone. Every year Sandy and I carry on as if we were characters in a Harlequin romance, acting out a formulaic gardening plot. At the first small intimations of spring, the growing season seems to stretch before us like a grand canyon of possibilities. We anticipate all the varied phases the gardens will go through, from the first brave bulbs of spring through the effulgence of summer to the last bright leaves of autumn. From the vantage point of spring, the panorama promises to be as unending as childhood summer vacations. But then, almost before we know it, the canyon has narrowed to the crack of doom, and the first killing frosts of fall have blackened everything. Where did the time go? we ask ourselves, bemused. Is this all there is to it?

Again elegiac poets raise their couplets for the occasion. So Samuel Johnson mourns in an ode to winter:

Life's a short summer, man a flower:
He dies—alas! how soon he dies.

And there it is in stark black and white: it is our own death that we see in the leaf-strewn soil. This isn't Harlequin, it's Bergman. The grim reaper stands at your doorway holding his scythe (which looks remarkably like the one you loaned to someone last year and never got back). Too late now anyway. Reluctantly you bid farewell to the daisy chains of childhood, the blood-red roses of love, the leafy bowers of sweet late-summer contentment. "Must I thus leave thee, Paradise?" you ask in bittersweet farewell.

Actually, not just yet. For one thing, all those leaves should be raked up and piled for leaf mould. And you know as well as I do that there's just as much work to be done in the garden in November as there is in April. So let's put away the hankies and get on with it. However, while we're on the subject of death, it would be prudent to give some thought to the whole question of what happens to our gardens after we've passed for the final time down their paths. As slapdash urban sprawl spreads across the countryside, destroying everything in its way, we see far too many lovely old gardens, long-neglected, scraped off the earth by bulldozers to make way for fried-chicken stands. The flowering border against which excited newlyweds posed for a photograph, the apple tree from which whooping children swung, the unruly honeysuckle rampant against a cottage wall—all of them doomed, all finally lost from time. Like many gardeners, Sandy and I make a point wherever possible of rescuing plants from abandoned gardens facing rude obliteration by the earth movers. This way, at least some bit of the magic of a place is retained.

Toronto garden writer Marjorie Harris maintains that a fine garden deserves to be preserved after its owner dies. "Every garden has something precious that should belong to the neighbourhood," she writes, "or to someone who will continue to appreciate it and share it with others." Harris advises gardeners to give a few minutes' thought to designating a plant executor similar to a writer's literary executor. I share these sentiments completely, but I can see trouble on the horizon: potential beneficiaries jostling for position to get their hands on your prized begonias. You just know how indignant your sister-in-law will be when she inherits that red hot poker she always passed comment on. And those wretched second cousins from Florida are sure to contest the will, as if they'd even know an astilbe from an anchusa!

No, I think the best plan is to keep on living for a bit longer, and this is something that gardeners are really good at. Some instinctive human wisdom instructs us that gardening is a physically and spiritually sustaining occupation. And plain common sense tells us that eating fresh produce grown in clean earth is apt to promote healthfulness. Now certain diligent but unhealthy-looking lab technicians are working their way towards the same conclusions: just the other day I read a news report about how scientists are experimenting with manipulating the aging process in laboratory rats by adding plant extracts to their diet. It seems that thyme (no puns, please!), along with oregano, celery, fennel, and peppermint, has high anti-oxidant properties that can forestall the breakdown of body cells associated with aging. Recent studies at the University of Sydney, Australia, show that garlic prevents cancer: 70 per cent of mice that were fed garlic and exposed to high doses of ultraviolet radiation did not develop any skin cancers, while 100 per cent of the animals not fed garlic developed cancers. (Precisely why we need to have creatures blasted with radiation to validate what every garlic grower knows I shall leave for you to determine.) Some among the jet set might look at gardeners as quaint custodians of an archaic lifestyle, but in our dotage we'll see who's worm-eaten and who isn't.

I didn't know it at the time, but when I put my old watch aside, I was leaving one dimension of time behind and entering another, the way the starship *Enterprise* warps across whole galaxies in seconds. Of course, my cheap Timex had nothing on today's high-tech timepieces. Trendsetters don't even have watches any more, they have chronographs, with tachymeters, countdown timers, compasses, and multiple time displays. These pawnshop specials resemble the control panel in a jetliner. Digital watches are the most heinous of all in my opinion, and I'm delighted to have never possessed one. I resent how they beep at their owners, scolding "Time's up!" Digital time stares at you insistently, inexorably, for a moment, and then disappears forever. At least the sweeping hands of my old Timex promised a return to the beginning, a comforting circularity and repetitiveness. Digital time, on the other hand, like the culture it clocks, represents a linear progression, a headlong hurtling towards oblivion.

The gardener plays an iconoclastic counterpoint to the frenzied tempo of our times, because the garden exists in circular, not linear time. The gardener plants by the moon and awaits the sun's warming of earth. Return and rebirth are the pith of our art. We move—albeit a little manically at times—through seasonal rhythms, through time that is curved. And we learn through time, through accumulations of insights. We develop a sense of our place in time within a long history and pre-history of plants, plantings, and plantspeople.

Linguist Max Picard writes about the difference between what he calls "divided time," which is chronological, measured time—the time people say they "kill" and "waste"—as opposed to "undivided time," which is the time of the spirit. Picard writes: "Love exists outside divided time and that is why lovers do not notice the passing of time, for in the undivided time of love there is more than they themselves can use." In their finer moments, gardeners exist in undivided time as well: you see them on the warm evenings of midsummer scratching away in their beloved beds, completely oblivious to the passage of hours, until darkness finally decrees it's time to stop.

3

Weather

To hear gardeners talk, you'd sometimes think their real passion in life is not for growing plants but for observing weather patterns. The garden itself seems cast in a mere supporting role, as a sort of fantastically elaborate weather cock by which to gauge the impact of the real superstar: climate.

On and on gardeners prattle: what a late spring it is; the wind is sucking all the moisture out of the soil; we need more snow to protect the rose canes. Their analysis suffers no half-measures, no moderation: this is absolutely the hottest or wettest or driest or coldest summer in living memory, the longest winter, the earliest autumn frost they've ever seen. New records for rainfall or rainlessness are set every year by their sketchy reckonings. Then, just as you think the conversation has mercifully run its course, some meddlesome old-timer will recollect the summer of '48 when it snowed in July, and that will set them all off again.

Most of this jawboning is by way of complaint. Gardeners view the weather, and the universe generally, as malevolent forces that exist for the sole purpose of wreaking havoc upon the garden. You know it as well as I do: transplant your tomatoes out in spring, after a painstaking hardening-off process, and a cold front is sure to come roaring out of the north that very night and blast the poor things to a sickly purple. Put out some brassicas, on the other hand, seedlings that love nothing better than a cool, moist spell during which to get established, and the sun will blaze down as though you were gardening in the sub-Sahara. Weather, gardeners conclude over time, is out to get them. This is the phenomenon that therapists refer to as horticulturo-climatic paranoia.

Not yet weather-beaten, the novice gardener may suppose herself to be standing on the solid ground of science. Here I mean the hardiness zones. One consults a standard text—for us it was *Wyman's Gardening Encyclopedia*—and is promptly directed to the "hardiness map," which neatly dissects the United States and Canada into ten zones based upon the average annual minimum temperature for each zone. Zone one, coloured on our map a pleasing forest green, is found only in northern Canada and can expect winter temperatures below minus fifty degrees Fahrenheit. Nothing is said about this zone's penchant for sudden forays southward. At the other end of the scale, the greyish zone ten— largely confined to the southern tips of Florida, Texas, and California—dips only to thirty to forty degrees F. Our Pacific Northwest garden falls into salmon-coloured zone eight, where expected lows range from ten to twenty degrees F.

Even the greenhorn soon realizes that, on a small-scale map such as this, it's impossible to show all the minute climatic variations within each zone. Wyman himself freely admits that "the hardiness of plants is based not only on a plant's resistance to minimum low temperatures, but to other factors as well, such as lack of water, exposure to wind and sun, soil conditions, length of growing season and, with perennials, the amount of snow cover during the colder winter months." With the variables mounting faster than a buck in rut, gardeners soon cultivate an unhealthy skepticism about these broad-brush zones. Whatever the warnings about hardiness, growers seem perversely determined to ignore them, and instead develop an exaggerated estimation of their own expertise in the matter of local microclimates. Even more dangerous is the gardener's recklessness in what is known as "pushing the hardiness zones." This manifests itself as an irrational desire to cultivate plants that cannot possibly survive local growing conditions. I think of it as a form of horticultural bungee-jumping.

"There is nothing like impossibility for getting a gardener's energies up," writes American author Henry Mitchell. My father is one of these types. A jaunty little

Irishman, he gardens in Ontario, which is where sinful gardeners should all be banished to in lieu of purgatory. Although nearly eighty years old, he still loves to trundle great potted tropicals out into the garden each spring and back into his crowded little house each fall just before the savage Ontario winter blasts everything in its path. From our privileged niche on the temperate west coast, we watch with perverse glee as gardeners in these cold-winter zones go about their autumn preparations: wrapping shrubs in burlap sacking, piling conifer branches over rose beds, heaping up leaves, earth, and salt hay, and generally carrying on as though another ice age were commencing.

Moderate cold and extreme dampness are the chief mischief-makers where I live in the Pacific Northwest. But these are not sufficient, for example, to deter the parks department of one nearby small city from attempting to grow a grove of palm trees. About a half-dozen little palms squat forlornly beside a busy roadway, never seeming to grow appreciably but never quite dying either. Over the winter, they're encased in protective wrapping and wooden crating so that they look rather like a row of corpses in upright coffins. But come the spring, they're still alive, by gosh, and get to spend another summer clinging desperately to life. This yearly cycle is held as a great success and proof of the region's balmy climate.

Not all gardeners are quite so barmy as this, but many are sorely afflicted. Take late winter. Anyone with any sense is in Hawaii or Mexico, reclining by a swimming pool, sipping margueritas under massed bougainvillaea blossoms. But not us gardeners. We've got our precious seedlings to tend to. In some households the fever commences before Christmas decorations are down. Seeds are sown in pots that are sealed in plastic bags and placed in warm locations all over the house. By February every windowsill in the place is crowded with anaemic seedlings. Mealtime conversations are dominated by long discussions of "damping off" and perceived breaks in the weather. By March the seedlings are leggier than a bevy of fashion models and the gardener is tempted to excavate a snow drift to ascertain if the soil is warming up yet. It's critical that the flats of seedlings have been accurately identified, because at this stage a tomato plant might easily be mistaken for a kiwi vine. As spring advances, gardeners keep busy by planting out tender annuals and trying to prevent their certain death in subsequent ice storms.

All too many of these grand designs for "getting a jump on spring" crash. Premature seedlings, if still alive, are jettisoned; there's a flurry of emergency reseeding, begun too late. Frantic, the gardener dashes to the neighbourhood garden centre and loads up on young plants whose appearance of astounding vigour, one knows, is a chimera produced by grow-lights and fertilizer force feedings, destined to disintegrate within hours of purchase. Throughout this comic opera the gardener continues to blame the weather for any setbacks encountered.

Most of the preseason hullabaloo has less to do with

the ultimate success of the resulting garden than with the gardener's compulsion to be doing something useful during the long stretch between ordering seeds from the catalogues and actually planting anything out. In our area May 24 is the traditional date for putting out plants susceptible to frost. Some local old-timers won't so much as set spade to soil before that watershed date, even though the spinach season, for example, is all but over by late May and lima beans should be halfway grown by then. Their faintheartedness is a symptom of people shell-shocked from too many years of being blindsided by the weather. It is prudence skewed to pusillanimity.

On the other hand, there's nothing quite so off-putting as the smug self-satisfaction of those who actually succeed in somehow cheating the cruelest months of spring. You know, the sort who'll invite you over for a meal of home-grown broccoli in April, and be eating ripe tomatoes before your plants have even set fruit. Invariably these overachievers have developed ingenious schemes involving greenhouses, hot frames, cold frames, and cloches. They will discourse on the intricacies of this infrastructure for far longer than required. It's not so much that the rest of us are envious of their picking fresh cilantro a full month earlier than we do, it's just that they can be so insufferable about it. Their false modesty can be annoyingly cloying. Secretly you suspect their methods. Their spinach, for example, seems always to suggest testosterone.

Back home, you're gratified to recognize in your own approach to springtime planting a fine balance between the extremes of unnatural haste on the one hand and fearful inertia on the other. Besides, you do eventually get some deserved recognition too, because springtime produces a veritable torrent of weather talk among gardeners, and it's particularly gratifying for plantspeople with established reputations to be consulted by neophytes. "Is it too early to plant peas?" one is asked. "Is it still too cold for cosmos?" Such enquiries should where possible be entertained out-of-doors, in full gardening attire, and preferably leaning on a spade or fork. The proper rubric requires that the expert scan the sky meaningfully, take note of the state of nearby native vegetation, and then quote something like the old Ontario pioneer farmers' adage: "Plant corn when oak leaves are as big as a squirrel's ear." Best results are achieved if you then resume spading purposively. When questioned by a New Age sort who wants to know if we're in the right phase of the moon for planting, a favourable impression can be created with a classic old rhyme such as: "Sow peas and beans in the wane of the moon / Who soweth them sooner, he soweth too soon."

A particular form of "cheating the seasons" endemic in the Pacific Northwest involves the planting of winter gardens. The idea is to have plants blooming all winter and casting exotic scents to enliven this gloomiest time of year. Of course, the real reason for doing this is to enable one to boast insufferably to friends who live in places that experience a real winter. I confess to having been seduced into this winter gardening folly. Off we went to the nursery and loaded up on winter-flowering plants. Foremost on the list was *Hamamelis mollis*, a large shrub known as Chinese witch hazel. Theoretically it produces an abundance of rich, golden yellow flowers with an exquisitely spicy fragrance in December and January. But not for us. Twice we've planted these wonderful shrubs and twice they've teetered for a year or two near the edge of death and finally expired. We're working on killing a third one now.

Our luck proved no better with *Daphne odora*, a small evergreen shrub that is reputed to produce rosy-purple flowers in February and March that are the most fragrant of any in the genus. Aware of Daphne's reputation for iffyness—its classical namesake was a tender nymph who had herself transformed into a laurel tree in order to avoid the clammy attentions of Apollo—we tended it with utmost solicitude. We examined it repeatedly, fussed over it compulsively. It too hung about for a season or two, producing a few dispirited leaves at the tips of its skeletal twigs. Rather than bathing us in wintertime fragrance, this puny ingrate dragged the stench of death through all the other merry seasons of the year. Eventually it died, and frankly, our bereavement was almost obscenely brief.

Even the winter bloomers that we haven't managed to kill off have been singularly unimpressive. A stout 'Pink Dawn' viburnum faithfully flowers in February, but the tiny and supposedly sweet-scented flowers have no fragrance at all. They resemble bits of sodden pink

Kleenex impaled on bare twigs. Another flowering shrub listed as extremely fragrant, the wintersweet, has developed into a rangy shrub of questionable manners that has declined to bloom year after year. We were at the point of ripping it out when we read that "experienced gardeners plant the shrub knowing that they must not expect it to produce flowers for seven years—and that even then they may be lost in a violent frost." Aspiring to experienced gardenership, we've let this malingerer hang on. But our winter garden is a thing of discontent, and those who live in ice-locked locations would do well to ignore the unseemly winter preening of West Coast gardeners.

Most gardeners like to have a few microclimatic tricks up their sleeves to cheat their nemesis. The harsher the climate, the more vicious weather's killer instincts, the more dazzling these stratagems. So you find certain craggy characters out on the Prairies, where nothing stands between them and the North Pole but a couple of barbed-wire fences, gamely training espaliered fruit trees on a north-south axis so that the north wind whistles right past. Other windswept growers put tremendous faith in microclimates created by walls, fences, and hedges that deflect freezing winds and trap extra warmth. These aren't people to be daunted by permafrost, and they're certainly not about to be intimidated by threats of premature thawing or winter sun scald. However, too many years spent in brutal growing conditions can induce in certain gardeners a brash combativeness, a refusal to acknowledge that their microclimatic cleverness has its limits. They become weather vain. It's disconcerting to encounter a seasoned grower in northern Saskatchewan seriously contemplating the cultivation of mangoes.

Less climatically challenged, we coastal gardeners have our own few modest tricks as well. At our place, a peach tree has to huddle under the eaves of the house to avoid rain-induced leaf-curl. A cluster of lovely blue alpine aquilegias thrives behind the north face of a large boulder in the rockery, safe from the scorching summer sun. We have a lot of stone retaining walls, and these are wonderful for creating particularly warm, dry, and sheltered pockets for fussy customers. For growing sweet peppers, eggplants, melons, and cucumbers—southerners that often won't produce much ripe fruit outdoors in our cool evening summers—we built a glass greenhouse, about three by four metres, attached to the house. The glass house also serves as a failsafe incubation chamber for sowbugs, white fly, and powdery mildew.

As well, we gardeners are inspired by an unearthly faith in new varieties of plants that clever hybridizers have developed for particular climatic conditions. A few years ago my attention was drawn to a tomato named 'Oregon Spring.' Distributed by a small regional seed house, it is custom-built for the cool-summer conditions of the Pacific Northwest. Splendid results were achieved with our first planting of them—an abundance of large, sweet tomatoes well ahead of three other varieties growing alongside. Here at last, we exulted, lay the solution to our pre-September tomatoless salads.

Much heartened, the following year we planted out dozens of Oregon Springs and cut back on the cherry tomatoes, 'Golden Queens' and 'Early Girls.' The summer developed into one of the hottest on record, a banner year for hot-weather crops of all sorts. But the 'Oregon Springs' decided to sulk. I've never seen a more stunted, wizened, disease-ridden, and generally bad-tempered bunch of tomatoes in my life. If fusarium wilt didn't get them, blossom end rot did. Their scabrous fruits hung green and peevish, while nearby vines of all varieties sagged with beautifully ripening fruit.

One learns not to question this sort of thing, nor to be too thrown off by it. As Henry Mitchell puts it, disaster is the normal state of any garden. Like storm-tossed castaways, we grasp at any bit of flotsam or jetsam, any horticultural straw that might save us from the tempest. In growing hardy perennials, for example, some people reject designer cultivars in favour of an "origin of species" approach. A trifle Darwinian, and perhaps too sensible for many gardeners, this stratagem involves seeking out plants that originated in a climate type similar to the climate where one lives. Plants genetically adapted to particular climate regimes, so the theory goes, will most readily adapt to similar growing conditions.

Thus, for example, our west-coast weather patterns match almost perfectly certain areas of the Mediterranean. The aubrietias that spread their springtime mats of mauve in our gardens with very little care, trace their ancestral roots to the mountains of Greece where the winter rain/summer drought regime is very close to our own. To find plants that will "naturally" take to one's garden and climate, the Darwinian gardener should first ask where the plants came from. The rest of us, however, can carry on labouring mightily to cultivate the ornamentals seen to such grand advantage in the estate gardens of Great Britain, where the climate doesn't even remotely resemble our own.

All of the foregoing—the fine talk about climates of origin, climate-specific cultivars, and contrived microclimates—is, in the final analysis, just so much bluff and bluster in the teeth of a gale. Certain things are predictable: if you fully intend to tie up the sweet peas, but postpone the chore until tomorrow morning, it's reasonably certain that hurricane-force winds will strike that night and flatten them beyond resurrection. On the very day that your herbaceous peonies begin to unfold their enormous double blooms for the wonderment of all, there's sure to be monsoon-level rains that will turn those many-petalled miracles into something resembling sopping pom-poms on chopsticks. Put the pelargoniums out in the warming days of spring and you'll draw down a killing frost from somewhere. Tardiness in cropping off tomatoes in the fall will fetch the same result. Ice and hail, wind and frost—the names of the devil are legion.

At the heart of our dilemma is the wretched unpredictability of it all. "Anyone who tries to forecast weather around here is either a newcomer or a fool," mutter local curmudgeons. Another of their well-worn lines is the classic "If you don't like the weather here, just wait five minutes." But you have to wonder if this unpredictability isn't a thoroughly modern phenomenon, because we've inherited a substantial body of folk wisdom concerning weather forecasting. "A red sun got water in his eye," predicts an old Newfoundland adage. "When muskrats build their houses high look for a hard winter," warns another old nugget; and another one says: "When the pigs run and play, expect a rainy day."

With neither pigs nor muskrats at hand, most of us depend upon the weatherpersons on the evening news. Once upon a time I maintained great respect for weather forecasters. I pictured them as retiring fellows with suspenders and bald spots who spent their days faithfully examining rain gauges and barometers. Their cautious and modest forecasts nevertheless rang with an authoritative accuracy. Nowadays their unpretentious dedication has been swept away in favour of the abrasive prattle of toothsome airheads, backed by satellite photos and computer simulations—in short, entertainers, who seem to specialize only in getting things wrong. In our part of the world there used to be weather ships permanently stationed out in the slosh of the North Pacific. Crew members, unless inebriated, were generally successful at describing the weather moving towards the coast. But the ships were scrapped in favour of satellites, and life has never been the same since. "Tomorrow it'll be sunny with cloudy periods," we're advised routinely, or cloudy with sunny periods. Meaning: expect anything from a hurricane to a heat wave. They can't even get the weather that has already happened right: "What a gorgeous day it was again today!" they'll crow, oblivious to an extended drought that has farmers, gardeners, and foresters down on their knees praying for rain.

As predictive reliability drops like rotten apples, there's a correlative rise in fantastic speculations about the cause of all this unseasonal weather. Volcanic eruptions are always popular. One of the locals will carefully put down his beer stein, wipe the foam from his lips with the back of his hand, and explain at length how the eruption of Mount Pinatubo in the Philippines has spewed an unbelievable amount of ash into the atmosphere and that's why the melons aren't ripening this year. Then somebody else chips in with a theory of how volcanic ash is actually compounding the greenhouse effect and contributing to global warming, so the melons should actually have ripened quicker. Everybody else nods, perfectly content with twin theories that hypothesize diametrically opposite results. Another home-grown climatologist then introduces the topic of El Niño as the real cause of our crazy weather. This periodic warming of the eastern Pacific, we're informed, triggers all sorts of erratic behaviour in air circulation patterns. Wintertime warm air pours up the Pacific coast and daffodils burst into bloom in February. But on the other side of the continent, the normal summertime flow northwards of tropical air—the Bermuda High—doesn't happen at all, so neither does summer. Much grumbling ensues. Drifting holes in the ozone layer put an additionally interesting spin on the uncertainty. Five minutes of thinning carrots in June and your skin starts to blister like a campfire weiner.

"The devil is busy in a high wind," says an old bit of folklore, to which late-staking gardeners mutter agreement. British folklorist Jean Harrowven writes: "Early man thought that storms were sent by weather demons and bells were often rung during a storm to frighten away evil spirits, while charms and spells were recited." The magical control of weather practised by ancient peoples using incantations, processions, and other ritual actions seems positively rational compared with our penchant for spewing out greenhouse gases and chlorinated ozone eaters.

Gardeners at least are advantageously placed for dealing with the escalating vicissitudes of weather. For example, deep down, most of us appreciate that a numbing bit of winter is good for the spirit. Lack of blackening frosts, we know, is a large part of the problem with southern California. Bud Grant figured this out long ago. Sports fans may well remember Grant as a very successful professional football coach, starting back in the sixties. He specialized in cold-weather franchises—Winnipeg in the Canadian Football League, then moving to equally frigid Minnesota in the National Football League. A square-jawed, grey-haired, joyless-looking fellow, Grant put such faith in the toughening-up merits of cold weather he wouldn't have on his teams any player, no matter how skilled, who hailed from warm-weather spots like southern California. In Bud's playbook there was no true grit to be found in soft climatic conditions. No matter how cold it was on game day, neither Bud nor his players could be found huddled beside the sideline heaters favoured by the wimps and losers his teams regularly clobbered.

In these times of increased climatic uncertainty, we gardeners could do worse than adopt the Bud Grant Hypothesis by placing our bets on tough and hardy players. In a word, plants more like ourselves, for nobody braves the elements with more bravado than the gardener. Insensitive to glacial cold and incandescent heat, the gardener potters about without even proper headgear. In monsoon conditions, when lesser mortals are vulcanized in raingear, the gardener's apt to be outdoors in a pair of broken-down bedroom slippers and an unravelling woollen sweater. Why not then cast our lot with similarly robust plants? Why not banish all those tender and half-hardy malingerers that require such massive infrastructure to coddle them through tough times? Let's forget dashing out into the October dark in a housecoat to throw blankets over some problematic pipsqueak that can't withstand a touch of hoarfrost. No more pouring whole reservoirs of water onto some frivolous exotic that wilts every time the sun shines. Let's go with more rugged native plants, tough customers and stout-hearted old species rather than mollycoddled hothouse cultivars. We'll laugh at the repeated blows of the climatic bully. We'll gaze with equanimity on the havoc wreaked by ice-storms and frost-heave, at the wind mauling the shrubbery. "Storms make oaks take deep root," we'll moralize in deep and authoritative voice.

Or am I dreaming? If we couldn't talk about the weather, grumble about it, blame it for our failures, praise it for our triumphs, compare it with previous years, consult the *Farmer's Almanac* and our own dog-eared weather records, hypothesize wildly about the causes of our increasingly crazy climate, what the heck would we have to talk about?

4

Soil

𝒯he very first garden that Sandy and I attempted, dewy-headed newlyweds at the time, was on the delta of the Fraser River. One of North America's great waterways, the mighty Fraser starts as a milky blue glacial stream high up in the Canadian Rockies, then flows south and west towards the Pacific, draining almost a quarter of the vast British Columbia interior. During the spring freshet, the river boils along, a muddy brownish grey, and each year carries some twenty-five million tonnes of sediments downriver, depositing them around alluvial islands and sandbars, in marshlands and mudflats at its estuary. The little honeymoon cottage where we took up married life squatted on the Fraser's flat delta lands, just south of Vancouver, land seized a century ago from the river and the sea by a rampart of dykes. Out back of our rented tumbledown shack, we solemnly broke ground and planted a vegetable garden.

Enthusiasm was our principal asset. We knew next to nothing about gardening, each of us having studiously ignored for years the gardening expertise of our parents, but as things turned out we didn't need to know much. We chopped off the rough turf, dug over the darkly rich, silty loam underneath, sprinkled various vegetable seeds around, and waited in the true bliss of ignorance to see what might happen. And what happened was astonishing: vegetables erupted out of the earth with astounding vigour. Cabbage heads swelled, substantial as bowling balls, and corn stalks surged skyward as if fighting for sunlight in a tropical rainforest. Several beefsteak tomato plants ran rampant up the white south wall of the cottage and onto the roof, three metres long at least, each setting a dozen or more trusses of enormous red tomatoes.

Hell, we said to ourselves in triumph, this gardening racket's a breeze, what's all the fuss about? Today, two dozen gardening years later, we've yet to duplicate the fantastic output of that first absurdly amateur plunge into "growing your own." For that effulgent first garden had almost nothing to do with our expertise or lack of it, and everything to do with the fabulous rich loam of the delta, produced over millennia by the Fraser's yearly depositions. Digging down into the ground, we'd penetrate through consistently black, moist soil, riddled with earthworms but with seldom so much as a pebble.

At less than a metre down, still in topsoil, we'd hit fresh water. Blessed with unobstructed sunlight from dawn to dusk and moist soil you'd sell your soul for, this was a garden where even eager greenhorns like ourselves could scarcely make a botch of it. We didn't know it at the time, but what we were doing in that little vegetable patch was a personal re-enactment of the history of agriculture, beginning in rich deltaic soils—the Nile, the Ganges, the fertile crescent of the Tigris and Euphrates—and eventually spreading out to more challenging landscapes.

Two years later found us freshly landed on a woodland acreage on one of British Columbia's Gulf Islands. Every bit the new pioneers, breaking ground for a vegetable garden that would underpin our vaunted self-sufficiency, we stuck spade into soil, anticipating the same sweet clean slicing through earth that we'd previously been spoiled with. Clack! went the spade as it hit a substantial stone just below the surface. Move over a bit and try again. Same thing. Eventually we laid aside our spades in favour of the grub hoe, a great heavy weapon of a tool resembling an outsized Visigoth's battleaxe beaten into a ploughshare. Swung above the head and driven down forcefully into the ground, it strikes against large boulders and tree roots with teeth-rattling impact. Boulders and roots there were aplenty in this raw piece of land. From dabblers in the fabulous soils of the delta, we'd descended to the level of horny-handed sodbusters.

Thus we learned one of garden life's self-evident truths: not all soils are created equal. Soil is actually a bit of a euphemism for the scanty overburden we unearthed at our new place. In searching out a piece of land to buy, we'd relied on instinct and, perhaps excessively, on time-honoured indicators of poor or productive soils. These indicator plants may vary from region to region, but I suppose the results are of similar value. Out our way, bracken fern theoretically thrives in poor soils while stinging nettles give promise of good fertility. Both were growing in abundance when we gave this acreage a cursory glance before following our instincts and purchasing it. Optimistic to the brink of naiveté, we chose to ignore the cautionary brakes of bracken and accept the encouraging evidence of stinging nettles.

Had we put as much faith in science as in folklore, we might have consulted the Canada Land Inventory agricultural capability map for the area. This would have told us that our little homestead was classified as having "no productivity" due to "bedrock near the surface" and "moisture deficiency." Would this have deterred us from buying a place that we'd loved at first sight? Not likely. A few grains of information are seldom sufficient to derail instinct under a full head of steam. Besides, "no productivity" is precisely the sort of challenge that gardeners everywhere take happily in stride. If planting a tree entails chiselling a hole through bedrock and filling it with soil and compost, so be it! One could do worse than spend one's life building up soil where nature has seen fit to build up none. We think of celebrated gardens created, like Findhorn, from wastelands. Today, after several decades of grinding labour, I've come to appreciate the fine irony of gardeners toiling away to enhance the productivity of rock heaps while another segment of *homo sapiens* is busily transforming gloriously productive areas like the Fraser delta into a miasma of freeways, furniture warehouses, and condominiums. Africa's most productive farmland, the fourteen-thousand-square-kilometre Nile delta, now receives only 2 per cent of the 100 million tonnes of silt deposited annually by the Nile before it was dammed. The breadbasket of North Africa for more than seven thousand years, the Nile delta is now one of the most heavily fertilized regions on earth.

It's remarkable how little attention many gardeners pay to the earth beneath their feet, despite its being the component most crucial to eventual success or failure. Oh, sure, we'll throw in a bucket of compost or manure on occasion, perhaps judiciously add a bag of peat or limestone when the mood strikes us, but we seem strangely reluctant to get very far down in the dirt and find out what's really happening. Perhaps a morbid premonition of the grave keeps us so determinedly above ground.

Noting our peculiar reluctance, gardening experts implore us to develop a soil profile. We tend to greet this sort of advice as though we were children being lectured about wearing rubber boots in the rain. Ho hum. But the experts persist. For one thing, they tell us, we can benefit enormously from having some notion of the history of our soil. Gardening where no one has gardened before, as

I am, this is a fairly straightforward matter. Our scanty soil is derived from the shales and sandstone that form this little island, along with whatever organic debris the Douglas fir forest has managed to accumulate over the last ten thousand years. There are no human skeletons buried here, no scandals or blood feuds or familial black sheep.

Digging over the potato patch on a dull day, I'll sometimes feel a twitch of envy for growers whose gardens reach back over generations and for whom a simple bit of spading can develop into a full-blown archaeological excavation. Strange artifacts come to the surface, stirring one's historical imagination. Old whiskey bottles might be a tip-off about rum-running, revenue men, and illicit gatherings in the garage. A ceramic doll's head dug up while lifting rhubarb roots could well whisper a merry tale of mischievous girls in pinafores and pigtails. An errant horseshoe hints of a long-ago bridle path, a spooked horse, a tragic fall, and a great romance dashed. And who do you think may once have chawed with that old set of dentures found mysteriously in the depths of the horseradish roots?

The experts advise us to excavate a large pit in the centre of the garden—something up to a metre square—and literally get down in the dirt to discover what's below the surface. Even the most disinterested among us will identify the topsoil by virtue of its being on the top, darker in colour than the rest, and seldom more than a few millimetres thick. Below lie the sandwich layers of subsoils and stones that provide important clues to future garden prospects—whether the soil will remain waterlogged or rapidly dry out, whether there's anywhere for feeder roots to spread or anything for taproots to tap. All sorts of surprises await: one gardener I know discovered an old roadbed running under his raspberry patch. Bottom-dwellers may hit groundwater uncomfortably close to the top. And gardens located on old farmland may be cursed with a tillage pan, a hard, watertight layer caused by too many years of tilling. Lying just below the tillage depth, it prevents ground moisture from rising up to the roots, and will block even vigorous tree roots from penetrating downwards.

Making careful note of all these impediments, the soil profiler next turns attention to the mechanical structure of the soil. Particle size dictates soil texture, and soil experts identify six categories of size, ranging from clay particles which are less than .002 millimetres in diameter, up through silt, fine sand, sand, and gravel. At the top end, stones are categorized as particles over thirty-two millimetres wide. Soil is always some combination of these along with organic matter. A fine sandy loam—highly desirable but seldom achieved this side of the grave—is at least one-half fine sand with a generous portion of silt and some clay mixed in.

The study of soil is called pedology, which always sounds to me like the name of a behavioural aberration involving feet. Mulling over the distinguishing characteristics of silty loams as opposed to peaty loams, the average gardener begins to falter in pedological commitment. You wonder if your time might not be better spent pinching out the new tips on the broad beans. But it's critical to know what soil combination you have, and the best way to find out is through the time-honoured "wash test." This is one of those procedures I haven't yet done myself, but don't hesitate to recommend to others. It entails simply taking a generous handful of soil, placing it in a large glass jar, half filling the jar with water and swirling the mixture vigorously. Eventually the various particles settle out at a level commensurate with their size: stones, pebbles, and coarse particles sink to the bottom, sand and silt are suspended higher up, and tiny clay particles remain at the top.

The results of the wash test in turn suggest remedial actions to be taken, which may help explain why so many of us decline to participate. To all but the most obtuse, a jar full of stones is self-explanatory, but excess amounts of clay or sand can often lead the gardener a merry remedial chase. In large gardens, the physical makeup of soil can vary dramatically from spot to spot. At our place, for example, I've identified three entirely distinct soil subzones. The predominant one consists almost exclusively of gravel, shale, and sandstone, suitable for pasturing mountain goats. In other areas, thanks to the caprices of long-ago glaciers, the earth consists of granite boulders about the size of basketballs embedded in sandy dust. Mixed among the movable cobbles are occasional massive granite blocks, called "erratics" and dropped by retreating icefields onto precisely those spots we plan to cultivate. With deceptively small visible tips, much like petrified icebergs, these monoliths, we've learned over time, are best covered up and ignored. In one smallish, low-lying spot there are no stones at all, just thick, heavy clay.

While the endless grubbing out and barrowing away of stones and boulders in the first two soil regimes is a tedious business, I still prefer it to dealing with the lumpish intractability of clay. You can spot clay-based gardeners from a great distance by their claggy boots and stooped posture. In my limited experience, clay exists in two states: stiff and ponderous when wet, and resolutely concretized when dry. It's a classic type of what the pedologists call "structureless soil"—so close-textured that neither air nor water can pass freely through it. The traditional remedy for opening up clay soils is to add sand in order to create pore spaces for air, water, and micro-organisms. Unfortunately, many of these traditional remedies suffer from the loss of certain vital specifics in the telling and retelling over generations, and this is a case in point. "Amend clay soil with sand," sounds simple enough, but beware! There's no mention of the beachloads of sand actually required. Pouring an insufficient amount of sand onto a clay bed can make matters worse rather than better, the sand particles performing the same hardening role amid the mass of clay as aggregate does in a concrete mix. You need one part sand to two parts clay if you want to end up with something more permeable than a concrete pad.

Beyond demonstrating soil's physical characteristics, the wash test serves another vital purpose in that it prepares the gardener for an even greater experimental challenge: conducting the home soil test. The soil-test kit has been called "the gardener's most important tool" in that it "takes the guesswork out of any soil-feeding program." Ignoring the fact that these claims are advanced primarily by people selling soil-test kits, Sandy and I, very early on in our gardening career, acquired a kit. It is designed to test soil for nitrogen, phosphorus, potassium, and acidity. Properly employed, it lifts the soil profile out of the pit of simply observing physical structure—this is a stone, this is sand—into the rarefied atmosphere of science. It helps one penetrate to the chemical core of the elements that compose soil.

Mighty nitrogen is the element we look to first, not just because it appears first in the numeric formula on fertilizer bags, but because the nitrogen cycle is vital to every living organism, governing plant cell growth and reproduction, providing the means whereby the blanket of nitrogen wrapped around our planet is magically converted into a form that plants can use, convert into proteins, and eventually pass on to animals such as ourselves. Whereas forests and other natural plant communities have evolved to a graceful and effortless participation in the cycle, cultivated plants wobble about like a child learning to ride a bicycle. Lacking sufficient nitrogen, a plant will suffer stunted growth and yellowing leaves. A nitrogen overload—invariably the work of the too-ardent gardener—will result in spindly stems, delayed flowering, and knobbly little fruits not worth the picking. Of the two extremes, nitrogen shortages are far more common, as this elusive element seeks constantly to escape from its landlocked state and disappear back into the atmosphere.

The instructions that accompany our soil-test kit assure me that the test for nitrogen levels is simplicity itself. You take the designated test tube, fill it one-quarter with soil and another quarter with the nitrogen solution provided, shake thoroughly, allow the soil to settle out and then compare the colour of the resulting liquid with the kit's nitrogen colour chart. The chart's spectrum of colours—ranging from maroon through orange to light yellow—indicates the minimum percentage of nitrogen needed to be added for a healthy nitrogen level. You then simply proceed to the nursery and buy a bag of fertilizer with the corresponding nitrogen number. What could be simpler?

Of course, it's wise to first check the levels of the other two of the elemental "big three," so we next turn our attention to phosphorus. Just as nitrogen's a slippery character, constantly seeking an escape route out of soil, phosphorus is problematic too. But its methods of resistance are entirely different: it locks itself up with other chemicals and refuses to come out. Taciturnity itself, phosphorus is notorious for digging in its heels and not budging an inch in soil. It absolutely refuses to move downwards, so that gardeners pouring bone meal or other phosphorus-rich fertilizers onto the surface in expectation of it filtering down to plant roots are wasting both time and money. Essential for good root formation and early growth, phosphorus has to be pretty well placed right beside the roots where it's needed, like a suckling babe placed to breast. Most of the phosphorus locked up in soil is never used, and there are now some urban lawns that, after decades of indiscriminate fertilizing, have so much phosphorus in them it's a wonder they don't glow at night.

Still, you can have phosphorus deficiencies, and established plants deprived of phosphorus will withdraw reserves of the element from their older leaves to support new growth. This leads to that perplexing phenomenon of a shrub producing reasonably vigorous new growth while its older growth withers and dies. Precisely the time for the home test for phosphorus deficiency, a test almost as difficult as the stubborn element itself. This time, after the soil has settled in the test tube, you have to stir the liquid with a pure tin rod for thirty seconds and then scrape the rod within two minutes. By now you're beginning to resemble an aged necromancer or a mad alchemist in the attic, but again a resulting colour, ranging on a spectrum from blue through yellow, indicates various levels of phosphorus deficiency.

After the truculence of phosphorus, potassium seems positively user-friendly. Third of the big three, potassium is not required in great abundance, but it's absolutely essential to a plant's ability to produce and transport sugars and starches. Slow but steady growth, vigorous roots, and a vitality that resists diseases and winter kill are among the benefits of ample potassium.

As well, this team player is a voice of moderation among the elements—for example, holding in check nitrogen's impetuous rush to produce too much soft new growth. Supplies of potassium can run low in exhausted farm fields or other impoverished soils, but are easily maintained in the garden by returning plant residues to the soil or through application of wood ashes or seaweed. It's so co-operative, one is almost tempted to skip the potassium soil test completely.

No such temptation ever enters the pivotal issue of soil acidity. Here now is the acid test of the gardener's commitment to pedology on the theoretical plane and to soil improvement on the practical. For centuries plantspeople have understood the rudiments of acid and alkaline soils. Here too, handy indicator plants provided valuable clues: sorrel would grow abundantly in "sour" soil, clover and alfalfa in "sweet." A primitive version of the scientific soil test involved the gardener or farmer actually tasting the soil: acid soil has a sour flavour, while alkaline soil is said to have a soapy taste.

Old-timers would talk about adding ground limestone to sweeten acid soils, and today the average gardener readily accepts that lime is a valuable physical conditioner of soil, that it benefits the activities of soil micro-organisms, and that certain plants prefer a slightly acid soil and others a more alkaline medium. Where we tend to lose interest, where some of us become positively irascible, is with long-winded discussions about flocculation and the chemical reactions specific to different points on the pH scale. The technical details of pH theory—including the erratic behaviour of mysterious players such as hydroxyl ions—just about require a Ph.D. in chemistry. Enthusiasts for this sort of arcana (few of whom seem notable for good gardens) will go on about how phosphorus and iron are only available to plants within a very narrow pH range, and how these elements get chemically trapped by aluminum compounds when the pH level drops below 5.0.

Not long ago I allowed myself to be stampeded by some of this chemical chatter. Certain of our acid-loving plants were yellowing badly—the so-called "yellow anemia" of chlorosis—and we concluded that a peculiar chemical imbalance involving iron deficiency was at the root of the problem. Off we went to a nursery and purchased a jar of iron chelate, an esoteric substance that supposedly offered a cure to yellow anemia. Back home I prepared to administer this wonder drug to a group of malarial azaleas. First I read the fine print on the iron chelate package: "This product is to be used where deficiencies, based on soil/tissue analysis, have been identified," warned the instructions. "It may prove harmful when misused." I paused. Of tissue analysis there had been none. Soil analysis had been confined to the questionable methodology of the home soil-test kit. Were there hydroxyl ions or free radicals fomenting chaos in the soil? Could I say with any certainty what the pH level was?

I could not. Several times previously I'd tested for acidity-alkalinity, but the results were at best inconclusive. I never once managed to produce in the test tube any of the bright greens or oranges of the test kit colour chart. My resulting liquid was invariably soil-coloured. All my results are like that. Testing for nitrogen, I don't get a bright orange or canary yellow, I get a turgid earthy brown colour that tells me nothing. Same thing for phosphorus. Even co-operative potassium balks when it comes to analysis, producing the same muddy brown results. I lay blame for this failure entirely upon my old high-school chemistry teacher, a manic-depressive tyrant whom we students secretly, and cruelly, called Fat Bob. In one memorable lab session, we were learning to boil water by holding our Pyrex test tubes of water over a Bunsen burner flame. Cautiously, I was holding my test tube too far from the flame for Fat Bob's liking. He seized it roughly from me and stuck it into the flame, whereupon it exploded all over him. "Must have been cracked," he muttered, wiping hot water and glass shards off his face, and I didn't have the stomach to tell him it wasn't a Pyrex test tube. I knew from that day forward chemistry and I should be at odds. My soil-test-kit instructions assure me that "anyone can use a soil-test kit—no knowledge of chemistry needed," but I know better. We still keep the old kit on a shelf in the far reaches of the pantry as a talisman of sorts, a gesture of respect to science and all the wonders it has wrought, but I sincerely doubt that I'll ever use it again.

Instead, as do most gardeners, I prefer to accumulate scraps of advice from respected sources who will validate my own unfounded theories. Clever American garden writer Frederick McGourty is excellent in this respect.

"The matter of soil pH is usually overemphasized, unless you happen to live on top of a bog or on top of a lime pit," he writes. "Generous use of limestone on moderately acid soil can do more harm than good to a lot of herbaceous perennials, especially the shade-tolerant ones." My thought exactly. And the same holds true for the incalculable complexities of trace elements—zinc, sulphur, calcium, iron, magnesium, boron, and all the rest. I appreciate that they're all important. I understand, vaguely, that too much calcium can trigger a magnesium deficiency and that too much magnesium can neutralize calcium; but deep down I don't really care. I'd rather rely on the sweeping generalities of hearsay—for example, it's taken as gospel hereabouts that our soil is deficient in boron—and respond accordingly. I'm gratified that most other gardeners do likewise.

Where I do find the stuff of soil to be really exciting is in the intriguing world of micro-organisms. "Soil is not merely a mixture of inert minerals—sand, silt and clay," writes Chicago soilmeister R. Milton Carleton, "it is a community of organisms that live in every pore of a soil mass....a handful of loam from your garden contains more living organisms than there are human beings on the face of the earth." Soil is alive, seething with untold billions of bacteria, fungi, protozoa, and other organisms. Sustaining this community, keeping it well fed, properly moist, sufficiently warm, and protected from harm is the real vocation of the gardener.

In this context, the gardener is something of a philosopher prince or princess ruling a vast empire that teems and seethes with industrious subjects. Their line of work is the breaking down of organic matter and minerals into products that plants can utilize. They are the fundamental deconstructionists. To take just one example, a particular group of bacteria works to transform urea—perchance made available by pouring a potty-full of urine onto a compost heap—into ammonium compounds. Further down the disassembly line, other bacteria convert the ammonium compounds into nitrites. Yet a third bacterial workforce transforms the nitrite products into nitrates that can be slurped up by plant roots.

This dazzling triple play is only one of innumerable processes occurring simultaneously within the soil. Other bacteria are busy fixing nitrogen from the air; still others form nodules on the roots of legumes which will supply nitrogen to the host plants. In death as well as life these uncomplaining legions serve the soil—as they die in their billions, bacteria and fungi release elements like phosphorus in a form that plants can use. By watering the soil and endlessly ploughing in new supplies of organic matter, the gardener is only indirectly feeding plants; more immediately, these are the life supplies of micro-organisms. If they lack sufficient organic matter or moisture, or get burned by chemical fertilizers and pesticides, these colonies of workers die out, leaving behind what we call impoverished soil, but what is in reality dead earth.

One of the great injustices that can occur in gardens is that earthworms end up getting a lot of the credit for work being done by micro-organisms. Earthworms are the chief executive officers among soil organisms, plump fellows who spend most of the afternoon at lunch while dutiful underlings back at the office stagger under a crushing workload. No doubt about it, worms are movers and shakers: Charles Darwin calculated that worms working in one acre of good earth will move up to fifteen tons of soil in a single year. The question is: to what purpose? Milton Carleton argues that earthworms, while doing some good, are overfed floaters compared with micro-organisms, that worms don't create plant foods, capture solar energy, or fix nitrogen from the atmosphere. All they really do is eat, and most of what they consume gets burned up as energy and passed off as carbon dioxide.

Beyond gluttony, the earthworm's primary function is to offer reassurance that one's garden soil is in good condition. Earthworms only live where the pickings are good. They won't move into poor soil and help make it better; they leave that sort of thing to the underlings. But if soil is already rich and moist and littered with tasty organic morsels, earthworms come wriggling in from who knows where. There are barren spots on our property where you could dig for days and never see an earthworm. And yet, if I leave a pile of freshly cut grass clippings on one of these spots, within a couple of days dozens of plump pink wrigglers will have taken up residence under the pile and be happily gormandizing on the grass.

A paucity of earthworms doesn't necessarily indicate impoverishment of soil. Earthworms don't like to be disturbed while they're eating, which is most of the time, so that areas that are frequently dug over, such as vegetable beds, may contain very few worms even though conditions seem otherwise ideal. It's important for gardeners not to succumb to feelings of inadequacy here. I'm a great believer in spading over our raised vegetable beds in spring and fall. The earthworms, I notice, avoid this hurly-burly by congregating under mulch along the pathways. There is a school of thought that other soil organisms similarly dislike being knocked about twice a year or more, and that they'd do better work if left entirely alone under a thick mulch. I couldn't agree more—if the soil is reasonably rich to begin with. If we were still gardening back on the alluvial flats of the Fraser delta, we might never set spade to soil at all, but merely pull back the mulch and plant. But in the impoverished sand and gravel of our present outpost, I think a wiser course dictates the systematic folding-in of compost and green manures.

Undeniably, some gardeners go to extremes, cultivating wet ground in spring and doing far more harm than good by compacting soil. Or you have those obsessive British types with their relentless trenching, in which the entire garden to a depth of two spade blades is completely inverted on a regular basis. Plainly mad, these zealots put their faith entirely in soil movement as the key to creating rich garden loam.

And that's what it's about in the end—working the

earth up to gardener's loam, that fabulous dark, moist, friable, organism-swarming soil that you read so much about in gardening books. We long for the crumbly good tilth that results from the correct proportions of sand, clay, and silt particles richly commingled with organic matter and wonderfully pungent with a strong earthy smell. Soil that drains perfectly and yet remains moist throughout the cruelest drought. Loam that's as airy as a good soufflé, full of pores and passages in which air, moisture, and beneficial organisms work their magical transformations. I can see it all now: the grub hoe and spade permanently retired to the back of the toolshed, the soil-test kit long forgotten, boulders banished, and earthworms aplenty. We'd lie about languorously, exulting as English playwright Douglas Jerrold did a century ago, that "Earth here is so kind, that just tickle her with a hoe and she laughs with a harvest."

5

Water

"*A* garden," chuckles the old joke, "is a thing that dies if you don't water it and rots if you do." Gardeners are an aquatic species, immersed in water, masters of sprinkling and spraying, mistresses of misting, splashing, soaking, and saturating. As water seeks always its own level, the gardener seeks repeatedly to come to equilibrium with this transient element. Plop a gardener down in a swamp, in some waterlogged bog, oozy and soggy, fit only for growing cattails and skunk cabbage, and there'll be drainage ditches planned before lunch. Put the same enthusiast in a barren land, a desert too desolate for lizards, where the surface of earth cracks and blisters from decades without rain, and just watch how long it takes for the hatching of some fantastic irrigation scheme.

Water gadgets abound. The garden shed is impassable with hose pipes and oscillating sprinklers, water wands, soaking hoses and sprayers, atomizers, misters, and other claptrap. You spot the real zealots out in the monsoons of March squeezing soggy handfuls of soil to test if it's dry enough yet for planting. Or standing in the desiccated debris of late summer, moaning like the prophet Ezekiel watering the scorched earth with his tears.

Less frequently, you run into people who appear to have achieved a dynamic equilibrium with water. Their soil is always moist but never poachy; their lawns glisten greener than a postcard from Ireland; you never catch them, as you're so often caught, with an unruly hose pipe curled like a python round their legs. These are people who have integrated themselves into the great water cycle, blessed souls for whom the water wheel of life turns smoothly. No acid rain falls on their parade.

I shall deal with these people shortly. But first I'd like to tell you my own story about gardening and water. It's a long and cautionary tale, and I press it upon you for the salutary lessons it has to teach. Those of us who live beyond the farthest reaches of municipal water lines, who are called upon to both locate a reliable source of potable water and deliver it effectively to the garden, know water tribulations that make the inconveniences inflicted upon the average gardener seem mere drops in the proverbial bucket.

Things began optimistically enough. When we arrived on this little island one glorious day in early April to begin our new lives as countryfolk, the tiny creek that splashes merrily through our property promised an abundance of fresh water. We didn't know at that time about "seasonal" creeks—a local euphemism for waterways that roar like Niagara throughout the winter and dry up entirely before summer. By May our torrent had subsided to a dribble.

After some deep thought, we decided to dam the creek, thereby impounding sufficient surface water to last us through the summer. We pry-barred, rolled, and wheelbarrowed huge rocks and boulders to the site. We smeared spadefuls of thick clay between and over the stonework. Enthused by the project, I began to entertain fantasies of developing a little hydroelectric plant—we had no electricity at the time—powered by the gush of water through the spillway. But by the end of May the gush was gone. The creek dried up completely and the impounded water soon seeped away into the earth. Alarmingly, we were beginning to experience the moisture deficiency the land inventory people had forewarned.

I consulted an old-timer. "Look to trees," the old codger said to me, "if there's cedar and alder trees growin', there's sure to be water in the ground." This is the sort of rustic lore an ambitious greenhorn swallows by the forkful. Thrilled by its folk wisdom, I selected a low spot in our little valley. All about me towered big cedars and bony alder trees. Seizing my spade, I excavated a large hole about a metre deep. There I hit hardpan—a sort of imperfectly formed stone, something like a hybrid of clay and shale. I broke this up with my grub hoe, flung it out of the hole and promptly hit sandstone, which passes for bedrock in these parts. I smashed and pried at it with a pickaxe, and in between its layers, there came dripping and trickling little streams of pure fresh water. I'd done it! I'd found water!

Within a day or two, water had filled the hole to half a metre deep. By now our newly planted vegetable patch was crying out for irrigation in the drying days of June. With the new well filling, we stood poised for serious soaking. And, perhaps most impressive of all, I'd developed a low-tech pumping system that consumed no fuel and generated no pollution.

Here's how it worked: rummaging around in a salvage shop I'd come upon a solid brass hand-driven pump; I think it was designed for bailing out navy lifeboats. You cranked a handle that turned a small sprocket connected by a drive chain to a larger sprocket that drove the pump. The chain is what sparked my right brain into one of those wonderfully intuitive flashes that are the stuff of genius. I bought the pump and hurried home. I scrounged a battered old bicycle from the island dump. Mounting both pump and bicycle onto a plank platform, I connected the bicycle's drive chain, not to the back wheel, which I'd removed, but to the compatible sprocket on the pump. By stationary pedalling, I would pump directly from the new shallow well up to our thirsty vegetables. Brilliant!

I stationed the pumping platform near the well and

primed the pump. About forty metres of black poly pipe stretched uphill from pump to garden. As luck would have it, a carload of city friends showed up just in time to witness this miracle of new-found rustic ingenuity. Sandy took up her position at the end of the pipe, ready to splash the water while I pumped. I mounted the bike and began to peddle. Sloshing and sucking noises issued from the pump. I picked up the pace, grinning with self-satisfaction at the admiring visitors. Gurgling and slobbering noises in the pipes. "Anything yet?" I called up the hill to Sandy. "Not yet," she called back gamely, "but I can hear it coming!"

I took it up another notch, and the old bike fairly rattled and clattered on its platform. The chain spun wildly. The little pump whirled and gurgled. "Anything?" I bellowed to Sandy. "No!" By now my legs were pounding up and down like pistons. I was pouring sweat, my lungs bursting. I bore down on the bike with the gritty determination of a Tour de France frontrunner. But from the corner of my eye, I could see the looks on our city friends' faces: concern, anxiety and, yes, undeniably, pity.

Eventually I gave it up. I staggered off the bike and up the hill on wobbly legs. "Didn't anything come out?" I gasped. Sandy, still holding the pipe in a splendid show of support, replied: "Well, there were a couple of drops..."

Within a week or two this minor humiliation dwindled in significance, largely because the new well went completely dry, leaving nothing to pump anyway. I consulted another old-timer. "Hell, that's just surface seepage you were gettin'" he told me. "You need to get a dowser in there and find a real spring." Of course. We'd read a bit about this dubious business of dowsing. Also called water witching or divining, it seems typically to be carried on by an elderly countryman who, using a forked green branch or a metal divining rod, can locate underground streams. Tales are told of how municipalities, having mislaid the blueprints for buried water lines, would in desperation call in a dowser who would proceed to locate with pinpoint accuracy all the buried pipes.

I have yet to hear a coherent explanation of how and why dowsing works. Explanations lean more towards magic than science. But this is entirely appropriate, because since ancient days wells and springs have been thought of as magic places. In pre-Christian times, spirits of the water inhabited them. Thus Jean Harrowven writes in *Origins of Rhymes, Songs and Sayings*, "Every river in Britain had its kelpie, every lake its monster and every spring or well its bogart or banshee."

Generally malignant, the water spirits were offered sacrifices, sometimes human, in payment for an assured supply of pure water. Crichton Porteous writes in *The Well Dressing Guide*, that the custom of dressing wells may have evolved from "the age-old fear and worship of water gods and spirits. Into rivers, springs and wells peoples of countries of the world over have at times cast virgins, children, choice animals and flowers as votive offerings for the gift of water, or as bribes against floods and drought."

As Christianity pushed out the old European nature religions, the wells and springs were taken over by saints, who banished the water spirits, and the wells were renamed for their new saintly patrons. In time, some of these wells became shrines, their waters imbued with healing powers. Pilgrimages would be undertaken to the holy wells, whose waters would be used in baptism and for healing. The miraculous spring at Lourdes in France still flows in this tradition.

During times of plague and pestilence, wells that continued to supply pure water were especially revered, because the countryfolk believed they had been spared from the plague through the pureness of their drinking water. Thus a chant about Saint Olav's well in Aberdeen-shire: "St. Olav's well low by the sea / Where pest nor plague shall never be." In our post-Christian times, many healing wells have been downgraded to the status of wishing wells. Throwing coins or pebbles into a pool to bring good luck is a re-enactment of a centuries-old custom whose origins lay in appeasing the pagan water spirits.

With our own hydrological expertise exhausted, we decided to suspend disbelief and bring in a diviner. Needless to say, you don't find diviners listed in the yellow pages. Theirs is no ordinary business, but one shrouded in the mists of pseudo-science, psychology, and semi-mysticism. Some will speak of their particular skill as a heaven-sent "gift." Some will refuse payment for their services, for fear of forfeiting the gift. As well, a suspicion of charlatanism attaches to certain diviners. One chooses one's water witch, it quickly became apparent, with utmost care.

We asked around, and eventually settled upon an elderly gentleman who lived down the south end of the island. We went down for a courtesy visit. Bill was a fine old chap who welcomed us in, delighted in showing us the hummingbirds flitting around his feeder and regaled us with all sorts of local gossip. But when it came to the matter of witching he grew wary. He suspected the gift had left him. He doubted his capacities. Unprepared for a dowser with an identity crisis, we built him up; we jollied him along; we professed tremendous faith in his powers. Eventually Bill succumbed to our blandishments and said he'd come "give 'er a try." But he made it plain: he'd offer no guarantees. If the gift had deserted him, we'd be taking our chances. Fine, fine, we said and scurried home triumphant.

Bill showed up a day or two later, cut a thin forked alder branch from a nearby tree, grasped each end of the fork in an upturned fist and began marching methodically up and down the clearing. Sure enough, at a certain point the stick began to twitch and tremble, then pulled down with a sharp twist. There it was! Bill marked the spot and checked it from another direction with equally impressive results. Next he took a thin straight stick, balanced it across his index finger near the ground and tapped it. The stick bobbed up and down teeter-totter fashion about fifteen times before coming to rest. "There she is," said Bill, "about fifteen feet down. Feels like a good strong stream." By now his self-doubt seemed to have evaporated. We thanked him enormously, presented him with a bottle of whiskey—a traditional payment, accepted with no apparent fear that it might cause the gift to vanish—and bid him farewell.

Once again I fetched spade and pick and grub hoe and set to digging. I fashioned a perfectly square hole just under two metres wide. Down through the duff and the subsoil I went. Down through the hardpan. Down into rock. After I'd penetrated to about three metres, it became impossible to fling the diggings out by spade. We erected a tripod over the hole with a bucket on a rope and pulley. I'd fill the bucket from my excavations and Sandy would haul it up, dump the spoils, and lower it back down again. By about four metres deep I was into unfractured sandstone and had to chip through it with a large steel spike and small sledgehammer. More and more time elapsed between ascending buckets.

Deep in the bowels of the earth, chipping away like some demented goblin, I'd look up now and then and see the blue square of sky high above. Gradually I took to wondering about the wisdom of this course. Even worse, I began to feel afraid. Not just afraid I'd never hit water, but that this ridiculous hole could collapse and bury me. I had no interest in making the ultimate sacrifice to appease any lingering water spirits, so I shored up the sides with planks and continued chipping.

Eventually, at about five metres, I hit a pathetic little dribble of water trickling through a seam in the rock. On subsequent mornings I actually had to bail out a couple of buckets of water before commencing the day's chipping. By now I was well below where Bill had predicted the strong stream flowed. Was this farcical little trickle it? Mercifully, the ordeal came to an end with news of somebody on a nearby island who had hand-dug a well through loose soil down about ten metres. The chap climbed out of the hole one day, and just as he did so the whole thing collapsed inwards. This I took as a sure omen and abandoned further excavation.

That second well always had just enough water in it to get us through summer—for household use, that is; it never contributed a drop to the garden. But for the seven years spent in a small cabin without electricity or running water, the daily ritual of lowering a bucket into the well and fetching up a pail of cool, clear water is one we remember with affection. Carrying each drop of water you need for the day provides a priceless lesson in the true worth of clean water. In hot weather, lacking refrigeration, we'd store our goat's milk and other perishables suspended in a bucket in the well's cool depths.

Later we had a backhoe come in and excavate a water hole in a swampy area far from the garden. We used a gas-fired pump to irrigate the gardens—a noisy and foul-tempered contraption that would lose its prime every time you turned your back. Ultimately, with the coming of wisdom and electricity, and with an improved cash flow, we had a deep well witched and drilled near the new house. Charlie the well driller banged and battered his way down for fifteen metres and up gushed ten gallons of water per minute at the driest time of the year. Thus at last, after so much aqueous angst, we experienced the thrill described by American garden writer Celia Thaxter in her 1894 classic *An Island Garden*: "[I] turned the hose with its fine sprinkler all over the garden. Oh, the joy of it! The delicious scents from earth and leaves, the glitter of drops on the young green, the gratitude of all the plants at the refreshing bath and draught of water!"

I drag you, kind reader, through this long odyssey for one good purpose: our wanderings in a waterless land form a handy microcosm for what's occurring on a global scale. It's no laughing matter to reflect that half the world's population lacks safe drinking water, and that waterborne diseases kill millions of humans every year, accounting for an astonishing 80 per cent of all the illness on earth. Untreated sewage, agricultural run-off, radioactivity, and industrial effluents are contaminating water supplies indiscriminately. A succinct description appeared in the *St. Louis Globe-Democrat* a few years ago: "Every time you take a glass of water from a faucet in St. Louis you are drinking from every flush toilet from here to Minnesota." Two centuries earlier, Benjamin Franklin wrote: "When the well's dry, we know the worth of water." Today, everyone agrees, the global water well is badly contaminated and perilously close to dry.

Well, almost everyone. The message hasn't quite gotten through yet in places like Palm Springs, where a vulgar ostentation of sweeping green lawns, fake waterfalls, and expansive golf courses tries to pretend that the aquifer upon which all this gaudiness depends is not ineluctably drying up. The average North American household consumes about five hundred litres of water every day—roughly what a resident of sub-Saharan Africa uses in six months. Extensively watered gardens can push this total far higher. In some areas, the summer months see over 50 per cent of home water use going to irrigate lawns and gardens. Beyond despair, what's a gardener to do? As a calloused veteran of dry water holes, I would argue that all of us, even those awash in an illusory surplus of fresh water, are now called upon to reverence the gift of water, not by throwing virgins down wells, but by implementing water-wise gardening.

Now there's naturally a lot of moaning and groaning when a spokesperson for water-wise gardening commands the spotlight at centre stage. We know that they're going to wring some terrible concessions from us about what we should and should not plant. Nevertheless, we do have to admit that these people have some good ideas. They're the ones who have been convincing southern Californians of the wisdom of planting schemes that dramatically reduce the need for water, promoting the radical notion that succulents and cacti make far better sense in a desert environment than do English-style lawns.

Now they're after the rest of us as well, suggesting that we design our gardens around "water zones"—areas with differing water requirements ranging from low to medium to high. A stone patio with a shade tree requires no water at all, whereas a lawn is at the high-water end of the spectrum. "Grass is the biggest water guzzler in any garden," warns the Water Conservation Coalition of Puget Sound. Reduce lawn areas and water less, advises the group. Where lawns cannot be replaced with groundcovers, as in play areas, experts recommend seeding some of the new perennial rye grasses which are far more drought-tolerant than traditional lawn seed mixtures. Where possible, plant low-water plants together, preferably in those parts of the garden where it's most bothersome to water. Thirsty plants can live together in a high-water zone where it's easy to get water to them, or, best of all, in naturally moist or shady locations.

One of the perks of becoming a water-wise gardener yourself is that it allows you to flounce around town with a tremendously inflated sense of moral superiority. Simply encountering a lawn sprinkler soaking sidewalks, driveways, and other wasteful places can give rise to an indignation of exquisite correctness. Sprinklers splashing away under the noonday sun, when half the water evaporates before it hits the ground, can excite paroxysms of disapproval. You're more than willing to inform anyone who'll listen that the only time to water is in the morning when moisture seeps into the ground and is used by plants during daylight growing hours. You brush aside suggestions that evening watering is equally beneficial, patiently explaining that too much water is lost through transpiration overnight while the plants are resting.

The wealthy and well organized within the water-wise caucus install automatic, low-volume drip systems. These allow for easy and efficient watering, delivering water right to plant roots where it's needed, saving the gardener hundreds of hours of tedious waterwork and allowing such unaccustomed luxuries as leisure time and vacations away from the garden. On the down side, these high-tech solutions result in a distancing from the primal act of pouring on water. I find that an hour or two of honest hose work provides a guilt-free way of being in the garden without really working up a sweat. As well, it gets you close to the plants and provides intimate opportunities to observe the progress of various aphids, cankers, and blights infesting them. You also get a chance to knock a lot of plants about with unwieldy hose pipes and to engage in spirited discussions with your companion about what does or does not constitute an acceptable torrent of water with which to batter plants. Aging hose pipes add to the fun, as every time you move them they develop a water-blocking kink. Whipping the hose about like Lash La Rue fails to unbind the kink but can decapitate nearby plants quite handily.

One of the surest ways to reduce water demand, we know, is to incorporate as deeply as possible into the soil an abundance of materials good at retaining moisture and nutrients. Compost, sawdust, leaf mould, rotted manure, and peat moss all have these properties, along with an uncanny ability to be in short supply when most needed. At planting time, the parsimonious gardener and the water-wise gardener can engage in intensely heated exchanges over just how much slush money is available for purchasing overpriced bales of peat moss torn from hapless bogs. The idea is to encourage plants to put roots deep into cool, moist soil and away from the parched surface soil of summer. Almost as miraculous in their capacity to reduce evaporation and keep planting beds cool and moist are surface mulches. At our place we use piles of grass clippings, spoiled hay, and seaweed for this purpose. Even flat stones or cedar rounds placed in the beds will hold some moisture beneath their surfaces. The old "dust mulch" technique of hoeing bare earth to reduce transpiration is better than nothing, but a poor second to good mulching.

Perhaps most important of all, and perhaps most difficult to practise, is water wisdom in the choosing of plants. There are hundreds of lovely species that require little or no watering once established. Native plants of the region provide a good platform from which to take the plunge—they've evolved over millenia to thrive on precisely the amount of water provided by nature in that area. If desired, these can be complemented with low-water-use exotics from all over the planet: Chinese witch hazel and Roman chamomile, Persian catmint, and Serbian bellflower, Shasta daisy and Powis Castle artemisia and scores of others. At home, we rely heavily upon drought-loving herbs like thymes, rosemary, and lavender, upon succulent sedums, as well as mulleins, and yarrows, and thistly things like globe thistles and Arabian thistles, all of which carry on merrily without irrigation through the driest summers. So do sturdy foxgloves and amaranths, dianthus and columbines and poppies of all sorts, undemanding daylilies, candytufts, and cotoneasters, self-sufficient Japanese anemones, euphorbias, and ornamental grasses like ribbon grass and blue fescue.

Still, even with this bounty of drought-tolerant plants at hand, the water-wise gardener may succumb to awful temptations. Not entirely satisfied with the fine effect created by these dryland commoners, the gardener begins to feel powerful urges to indulge in a few plants that demand heavier watering. Perhaps a hairline crack in the dyke of common sense begins with a passion to have clematis climbing over everything, most of which really do like a good soaking now and then to keep their roots cool and moist. Like a reformed smoker indulging in "just one" cigarette, you next are tempted by herbaceous peonies, which also exact a certain water-toll as payment for their outrageous beauty. At this point prudence raises her voice, suggesting that you draw the line here. But soon you find yourself besotted by the lush foliage and clear yellow blooming spires of ligularia. You know that this is recklessness of the most reprehensible sort, that ligularias want their toes moist most of the time and are best left to people with waterlogged earth. But poor prudence is ignored again. Once onto this slippery slope, there's little hope of getting off. Pretty soon you find yourself lusting after a *Gunnera chilensis*, whose huge, rhubarb-like leaves are the largest that can be grown in temperate gardens, spreading up to two metres across and consuming water by the tanker load. With self-discipline fled, self-respect soon follows and in no time at all, the water-wise garden is undone.

"A lake is the landscape's most beautiful and expressive feature," wrote Thoreau. "It is the earth's eye." Just through the woods from where we live, a three-minute walk away, there lies a perfect small lake, known locally as "the beaver pond," which I think Henry David would approve of. Surrounded by tall conifers, a haunt of bald eagles and great blue herons, it's a Waldenish sort of place. Floating in a little punt among the water lilies, alone but for a querulous kingfisher, one can entertain sweeping thoughts about wilderness and civilization and the ultimate meaning of life.

With such a place at hand, you'd think anybody would be content to leave well enough alone. But the gardener is never one to drift indolently in the bosom of nature when there's an opportunity for back-breaking work to create a similitude of nature. And so we determined to create a "water feature" in our garden.

Non-gardening observers might shake their heads in incomprehension here, but the gardener is quick to defend these wild compulsions with the heavy evidence of history. For as long as there have been formalized gardens, something over five thousand years, water has occupied a central place in their design. The earliest gardens of pre-dynastic Egypt were founded upon the fruitfulness of the oasis, and made spiritual connection with the River of Life. Throughout the ancient Near East, the gardens of the wealthy were designed around irrigation channels that carried water to geometrical beds and eventually were developed into formal pools. In the Persian *glorieta*, flowing water linked and unified disparate planting areas. The Moors carried this centrality of water in garden design through North Africa, into Spain and Italy.

The flowing waters of the Persian paradise garden spread eastward too, into the great gardens of India. In the ancient gardening traditions of China and Japan, water, in pools and cascades, streams and fountains, is an essential element of design. When water was not available, a dry streambed of pebbles might be used to suggest its presence. In Oriental gardens, the shape of ponds is a matter of exquisite care, with bridges and stepping stones connecting tiny islands, and special viewing points from which to contemplate particularly pleasing scenes.

The sanctimoniously practical fish ponds of mediaeval monastic gardens, the phallic grandeur of geometric canals in French formal gardens, the improbably serpentine lakes of misty-minded English landscape architects, the chlorinated glory of the California swimming pool— each in its way pays homage to the time-honoured place of water in the garden.

Inheritors of these lofty traditions, and notwithstanding the natural beauties of the nearby beaver pond, we set to work on our own modest waterworks. This began harmlessly enough with further tinkerings on the little seasonal creek that had so betrayed our first irrigation attempts. Now we had a backhoe rumble in and excavate a small pond in the creek bed and create a dam with several huge boulders. Nowadays you'd be drawn and quartered for tampering with a natural watercourse this way, and rightly so, but back then nobody seemed to mind, and we didn't know any better. Throughout the winter rainy season, the creek cascades jubilantly over the rock dam and into the pond. One of our favourite winter thrills is to take a "sweat" in a small sweat-house near the creek and then emerge and plunge our over-heated bodies into the frigid waters of the creek, shrieking in exquisite agony.

Around the pond we planted ferns and willow trees, yellow-twigged dogwoods and black bamboo. A small wooden bridge crosses the creek and beckons one into the forest beyond. In early spring, when new growth glistens and pale sunshine glints on the pond's surface, it is a place of artless beauty. As the creek runs dry in early summer, the pond level slowly drops until by September it resembles one of those African water holes where herds of wildebeest mill around in the mud looking for a drink. But in place of big game, our little mud hole supports dozens of frogs and salamanders. As the water level drops over summer, the frogs crowd ever more closely together, until by the end dozens of them huddle in the mud around the remnant pool as though they were forlorn drinkers waiting stoically for the neighbourhood pub to open. When the skies do finally open in October and the rains come down with a vengeance, the pool quickly refills, the creek recommences its almost-forgotten gurgling, and we know that winter has officially begun.

A summertime mud hole wasn't quite what we had in mind for the garden. We were thinking more along the lines of garden writer Louise Beebe Wilder's description where "falls a garrulous trickle that threads the heat of summer days with a strand of freshness and relief and breaks in upon our consciousness with a sense of gay companionship." This sort of lyrical description is responsible for no end of gardening folly, and so it was with us. We decided to construct an artificial pool and cascade in the rock garden. Announcement of this plan roused a flurry of eyebrow-raising among acquaintances. "What, you're going to build a *phony* waterfall?" sniffed one, dripping more disapproval than we planned to drip water. We parried such comments with a stiff lecture on the role of water in gardens sacred and profane from time immemorial. Even more importantly in the social scheme of things, Sandy's father had several years earlier constructed a lovely backyard miniature cascade and pool; successful execution of a comparable feature in our yard would, I considered, provide both father and daughter with irrefutable evidence of my worthiness. And so to work.

Of all the gardening projects I've turned my hand to, none has seemed quite so daunting as the building of this problematic pool and cascade. The place was perfect: a natural hillside beside the house and deck. The scale was appropriate: a modest trickle cascading in a series of small waterfalls over a distance of perhaps five metres into a small pool two metres in diameter. The materials were at hand: generous blocks of native sandstone out of which the surrounding rock garden is also fashioned. The spirit was willing, and the flesh was too. But still I hesitated. I seemed becalmed by the very essence of the undertaking, by trying to capture that elusive element, water, and make it behave according to human plans rather than its own wild wanderings. Combining water with the electricity needed to power the cascade's circulating pump seemed to me fraught with peril, as foolhardy as balancing an electric appliance on the rim of one's bathtub. And in order to harmonize with our gardens, the cascade and pool needed to appear "natural" rather than a product of human artifice. By this point, I knew, Thoreau would not be approving at all.

Additional research seemed in order. But in the matter of designing and constructing water features, the experts are badly divided, their advice contradictory, their various opinions forcefully articulated. One tells you that a pool and cascade can be thrown together on a Saturday afternoon before the football game begins. The next commentator terrifies you with lengthy descriptions of enough rammed earth and reinforced concrete to support the World Trade Center.

Eventually, after what seemed like months of careful planning, decision-making that might daunt a grand master in chess, monstrous heaving-around of rocks and dirt, mixing of cement and experimentations with spillways, we got the thing done. We plugged in the submersible pump. We waited, trembling with anticipation, and yes, there it came: a tentative trickle, then stronger, growing to a boisterous splashing and gurgling, a playful, exuberant, lovely little cascade whose sounds tinkle and whisper throughout the garden.

The cascade threads its way through a miniature garden of mosses and ferns, dwarf conifers, and various alpines. The small pool at its base is edged with creeping Jenny, several varieties of hosta, London pride, and silver dead nettle. In an adjacent shady rock grotto we planted a bed of soft Irish moss. The idea is to recline here lazily during the long days of summer, reading a novel, sipping on cool drinks, soothed, refreshed, and rewarded by the sweet, cool splash of water.

Unfortunately, just as you're getting settled on the moss, a couple of problems crop up. One is that a certain amount of water loss, from splash and evaporation, is inevitable. No matter how minor the loss, it does not sit well with the water-wise gardener. Leaks are suspected. In lieu of poolside indolence, you end up prowling about, obsessed with plugging leaks you can't find.

Then the cascade gradually stops running altogether. You look for an obstruction, but there is none. You fish out the little recirculating pump and find its intake clogged with algae. Experienced water gardeners know that pool algae are not so much a problem as an opportunity. They are to pool owners what black spot is to rose growers; that is, an eternal conversation piece. Pool people can discuss the existence of algae, the control of algae, the aesthetics of algae, long into the night. In the best of all possible pools, algae are controlled through a delicate balance of pool-dwelling flora and fauna. Finding that point of equilibrium—perhaps adding a few more algae-grazing snails, possibly reducing the amount of floating duckweed—requires a wholesale commitment that largely precludes novel reading, extended drinking, or any sort of reclining.

After several decades of dealing with drought, dry wells, cantankerous water pumps, and leaking pipes, I've achieved a certain equanimity in the matter of water. This allows me to accept with good grace the realization that all the time, energy, and water we save through water-wise gardening is simultaneously squandered on operating this frivolous pool and cascade. It's called going with the flow, and I think of it as a reasonable way to appease the local bogarts and banshees, who have plainly played me for a tool ever since the episode with the bicycle.

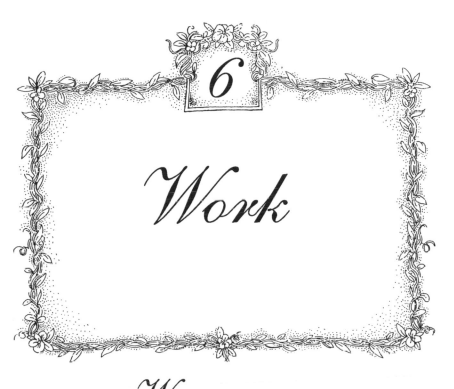

6

Work

$\mathcal{W}$e were slogging away in the gardens on a soggy late October afternoon. The soil was too wet to be successfully worked. Our gumboots stuck and slurped, our sodden work clothes clung uncomfortably. Stopping in mid-stride, a bucket of forlorn-looking daylily roots clutched against her hip, Sandy asked me poignantly: "Why do we think this is fun?"

This is a question no sensible gardener poses out of season. Yes, there are occasions during the growing year on which it is appropriate to speak of fun, perhaps of joy, even of love. These are the unmistakable instances, vivid but fleeting, when the garden blooms at a momentary pinnacle of perfection, brief epiphanies when no disaster looms, no earlier miscalculation leers. The world appears suffused with glory, cherubim and seraphim seem to sing, and the gardener is lifted spiritually into celestial realms of nectar and ambrosia.

For the rest of the time, the gardener's lot is a love of labour. "A thing of beauty and a job forever," grumbles one old definition of a garden. An editorialist at the *Baltimore Sun* put it cleverly: "The objection to gardening is that by the time your back gets used to it, your enthusiasm is gone." And old Ralph Waldo Emerson condemned the whole mad undertaking: "A garden is like those pernicious machineries which catch a man's coat-shirt or his hand, and draw in his arm, his leg, and his whole body to irresistible destruction." Caught in the maw of the machine, doing dirty work on a filthy afternoon, one dare not pause to ask, even rhetorically, if this is fun. Fun is for people who frolic at amusement parks and beaches and baseball games, not for gardeners.

The labour of gardening is aggravated by its wretched inescapability. Tulip bulbs demand to be planted before freeze-up, and you postpone the task at your peril. When leaves fall, the rake begins to rattle, like a house-bound dog demanding its walk. Through the seasons, supposedly helpful garden columnists are particularly annoying in harping on what chores need doing. Perhaps it's early spring. You've got your seeding work to do indoors, which is more than enough to keep you occupied. But the helpful experts won't let you off that lightly: time to get your hot beds and cold frames cleaned out and in good working order, they advise. On warm spring days, we're urged to get outdoors and start removing old leaves and trash from lawns and garden plots; be sure to carefully examine herbaceous borders and rock garden plantings for frost heave or other winter damage—list and purchase replacements, if necessary; it's time now to be dethatching, liming, and fertilizing lawns, and preparing ground for new lawn plantings; wooden arbours must be repaired and painted before the climbing vines break bud; while you're over there, why not prune out and retrain the clematis and honeysuckles? And since you've got the secateurs out anyway, better cut back some of the old wood on the trumpet vine; young Virginia creeper and wisteria need to be pruned now too; and the Boston ivy desperately needs a bit of a trim. All the roses and fruit trees absolutely *must* get their last dormant oil/lime sulphur spray now or they'll break bud and it'll be too late. The overwintered parsnips should be dug out before they start to grow new tops and are ruined. And, of course, now's the time to be cutting scions for top-grafting fruit trees. And on and on and on.

The gardener staggers about, wobbly-legged and weary, but there's no respite. Chores pile on top of chores in a perverse inversion of the domino effect: you can't plant the tulips until you lift those hardy asters and divide the clumps; but you were going to put the asters behind those 'Autumn Joy' sedums, and there are a couple of purple coneflowers that will have to be moved out of the way first; however, you've got nowhere to put the coneflowers—maybe you should clean off the annual bed and heel them in there; except that you wanted to turn the old compost heap before starting a new heap with the gatherings from the annual bed, so perhaps you should go turn the compost first. Then a discussion erupts with your companion as to why you're even thinking of wasting precious time turning compost heaps when all these damned tulips need planting!

The seasonally driven chores—all the transplanting, spraying, staking, pruning, layering, grafting, thinning et al.—jostle for your attention with ongoing infrastructure maintenance: the gate's off its hinges, the rose arbour is beginning to list precariously, that spiteful lawnmower has thrown a rock through the greenhouse, and water pipes can always be counted upon to spring a leak just when you're at your busiest.

Harried gardeners have a grand propensity for casting themselves in the role of victim. We like to picture ourselves as the playthings of capricious fate, unjustly overloaded with unlooked-for labour. We are in denial. We cannot admit openly what acquaintances gossip about behind our backs: that we are chronic workaholics. We have a weakness for work. We go willingly, exultingly off to the gulag. What to the outsider looks like irksome drudgery is to the gardener a labour of the greatest love. If growers were to have a motto, it might be Virgil's "Labor omnia vincit"—labour conquers all things. Or perhaps we'd adopt the venerable Benedictine saying, "Laborare est orare"—to work is to pray.

Gardeners are heirs to the holy notion that we work out our salvation on this earth by digging it up. We agree wholeheartedly with Thomas Jefferson that "those who labor in the earth are the chosen people of God." Who is more devoted than the gardener to the great Protestant ethic of diligence and frugality? Bankers by comparison are hedonistic wastrels. Like sour-mouthed Calvinists, we turn against the spontaneous enjoyment of life. Instead, we fire up the rototiller, vigilant against undisciplined impulses to enjoy the company of others, to engage in idle chatter, to take a siesta. In short, to waste time. We sniff the aroma of steaks being barbecued by deluded pleasure-seekers two doors down, and redouble our snipping of deadheads.

But not for naught. We gardeners may be hopeless drones, but we're a far cry from those Japanese executives who succumb to *karoshi*, or death from overwork. Garden work accomplishes the exact opposite: it reduces stress, defies fatigue, and lengthens life. Not long ago I encountered an ancient Mennonite couple—they were both well into their nineties—working vigorously in their vegetable patch. Of course, they were beginning to slack off a bit: when it's time for extra-heavy work, such as digging over the potato beds, they have their kids, who are mere striplings in their sixties, come in to help. Long after the beer and baseball crowd has gone to the everlasting dugout, the gardener is still puttering away.

A study of this subject was conducted at Kansas State University by a group of academicians calling themselves "horticultural therapists." These scholars divided their study subjects into two groups, one of which was given the task of sorting paper while the other group worked at mixing soil and potting plants in a greenhouse. Measuring classic indicators of stress, such as pulse rates, blood pressures, and skin respiration levels, the researchers found that stress levels were consistently lower in the group doing gardening work. Even more dramatically, a study at the University of British Columbia compared the rate of violent incidents at various intermediate care facilities housing Alzheimer's disease patients. Over a two-year period, the study showed, violent incidents dropped by 19 per cent at facilities with gardens, but increased dramatically at those without gardens. Workaholics we gardeners may be, but at least we're docile workaholics.

Up to a point, that is. Gardeners, like other mortals, have a breaking point. Often the crisis arrives during the "dog days droop"—that appalling late-summer period when everything that was recently fine and beautiful in the garden is now dreary and desiccated, when grotesque gaps are revealed in the planting schemes, when pests and parasites multiply faster than amoebas, and one's energy drains away like water on earth too dry to be moistened. Few personal encounters are more unnerving than meeting up with a gardener who has temporarily lost her grip. Where in April all was vibrant energy, now a dull lassitude besets her. "Oh, what's the use?" she asks from a turgid pool of lethargy, and we can find no suitable answer. It's particularly disconcerting to encounter such defeatism in one we had previously thought indefatigable. Such cases require immediate removal from the gardening environment. Recovery may be induced through rapid immersion in synthetic surroundings: shopping malls, office towers, and airports are all excellent. In a pinch, parking lots or parkades may suffice. Generally, a few hours spent in such surroundings will restore the gardener's spirits, and even an incontrovertibly disastrous garden will begin to look pretty good.

What's regrettable is that just a bit of foresight could have removed any need for radical shock therapy. It's astounding, for example, how little attention many gardeners pay to the keystone role sound planning plays in reducing garden labour. At our place we've made a real point of always locating compost heaps at the furthest possible distance from where their compost might be required. To fetch a barrowload of compost for top-dressing the roses in spring just about requires an overnight expedition. Similarly, our tool shed possesses the charm of remoteness. Entire afternoons can be spent trekking between garden and shed in search of implements.

Experienced growers never tire of telling us that one of the most important features of a low-maintenance garden is ease of access to its plants. Convenient footpath layout and inclusion of access corridors, such as a catwalk along the back of a border, will, we're told, cut the workload dramatically. This advice we ignore on principle. Far simpler to crash one's way through the undergrowth, trampling wayward plants as one goes. In the same vein, we're enjoined to avoid gardening projects that automatically entail intensive care—features like rock gardens, about which Henry Mitchell writes, "nothing known to man equals a rock garden for labour." But you're not daunted by the prospect of a little work, are you? So in goes the rock garden, and there goes your life.

We're advised to develop low-maintenance planting schemes by first carefully pondering the requirements of individual plants, and then selecting species that will more or less look after themselves. We all nod our heads solemnly, and then proceed, like willful children who make a point of doing the opposite of what is requested, to load up on irises, roses, peonies, and delphiniums, all of which will require endless staking, caging, pruning, tying, spraying, deadheading, and regression therapy. Not to mention moving. The chronic moving of plants is a classic symptom of a gardener gone over the edge. I'm thinking here of people like Sandy's stepmother, Agnes. A wonderful gardener, she's also an inveterate mover. I'm not referring to your everyday moving of pygmy plants from the background to the foreground and shoving giants to the back. Everyone does that. But perfectionists like Agnes will dig out—or have a suggestible son-in-law dig out—a huge rhododendron, one of those brutes with a rootball the size of the family car. We'll wrestle it out and eventually replant it in the same bed, so it ends up about twenty centimetres from where it started. "There!" Agnes will exclaim, standing back like Michelangelo in the Sistine Chapel, "that's so much better!"

Most of us are not like this. Most of us are what I call "good enough for now" gardeners. We specialize in doing jobs just well enough to get by for the moment. Always on the grounds that we're too busy just now to take the time to do them properly. I like to think of us as disciples of the ancient Greek philosopher Heraclitus, who taught that all things are in flux. I'll give you an example: along the driveway into our place I planted a row of mountain ash saplings. Standing outside our fenced gardens, the little trees required protection from omnivorous deer, so I provided each of them with a round cage, 1.5 metres high, fashioned from galvanized stucco wire. Plenty good enough for the moment.

A permanent solution would entail driving a tall stake into the ground and affixing cage to stake in such a way that the cage can be easily detached for plant maintenance and readily reaffixed. For a multitude of perfectly valid reasons, I never quite get this far. When winter southeasters come thumping up the Strait of Georgia, my cages topple over, bending the saplings with them and often scraping off buds, bark, and new growth in the process. Hurrying past after the storm, I take a moment to set the cages aright, straighten the little trees, cluck over the damage they've suffered, rail against the perversity of natural elements, vow that I shall properly stake the trees tomorrow, and dash off on the errand of the moment. Over the years I've expended several times as much effort in shoring up my temporary solution as would have been required to do the job properly in the first place. Maybe tomorrow. "Good enough for now" gardeners possess a legendary capacity for accomplishing more tomorrow than they ever do today.

Undersized stakes are a particular favourite of disciples of Heraclitus. The methodology is disarmingly simple: for any plant that requires staking, always select a stake that will be too short to support the plant properly but sufficiently close to tall enough that it justifies your not replacing it with a taller one. Take the case of several jaunty little contorted willows that I'd raised from softwood cuttings. I had plenty of time for admiring their crazily twisted growth pattern, but never a spare moment to replace the skinny little sticks to which the whips were lashed. Over a metre high, and tied around their knees to a chopstick, the poor trees whipped around in the wind so much they took contortion to levels Houdini never dreamed of.

No amount of previous experience seems able to dissuade us from our staking shortfalls. I go through it every year with delphiniums. Lots of people have trouble growing delphiniums, but for some strange reason they grow splendidly at our place. Graceful, elegant, effulgent in their lovely pastel blues and mauves and whites, they regularly tower well over two metres high. A wise gardener would seize upon these beauties as a mainstay of the June garden and do everything necessary to ensure that they're displayed in their full magnificence. Such is not the way of the true Heraclitean.

Delphiniums require staking, there's no argument about that, and staking has, in the mysterious ways of such matters, fallen into my job description. I don't begrudge it; indeed, I tackle the chore with considerable gusto. Two elements only are missing: getting it done early enough, and using sufficiently tall stakes. My method gets me out there when the plants are about two metres high and bushing out blowsily. Traditionally I use stout yellow cedar stakes, two metres long, pounded into the ground with a sledgehammer. One consequence of doing this chore long after it should have been done is that the bushiness of the plants, besides tangling up the sledgehammer, often obscures the roots, with the result that I may pound the stake right through a root crown, thus permanently crippling the plant. Another helpful tip is to always use fewer stakes than are actually required, which contributes greatly to the disastrous effect eventually achieved. The stakes, once driven in, look a bit ungainly but are strong enough to withstand stampeding elk. I loop twine around the delphiniums and connect it stake-to-stake. Choice of twine is also important: my preference is for old twine salvaged from hay bales, that bright orange stuff, which gives the entire production an unremittingly rustic look.

In the fullness of time, the delphiniums tower above the stakes and their lush foliage all but obscures the unlovely infrastructure. Then they begin to list. Eventually their heavy flower heads take an interesting semi-horizontal position, as though they were practising kundalini yoga. At this juncture, discussion commences as to the inadequacy of my initial staking work. Abandoning other projects, not always with good grace, I hurl myself into a remedial plan of action. This involves lashing three-metre-high bamboo canes to the cedar stakes. The horizontal flower heads—such perfection of beauty!—often exhibit a marked disinclination to resume a vertical position. Force is applied. A few stalks snap off completely. A curse or two might ring out. The surviving stalks get rather roughly bound to the bamboo canes. This is not a pretty sight.

Unhappily, what the supplemental canes add in height they lack in strength. Within a few days the weight of the sumptuous flower heads—usually increased by a torrential rainfall about now—begins to bend the bamboo. More string is strung; guy wires are run out to nearby trees and shrubs. In the end what might have been a magnificent display of blossoming spires has been reduced to an undeniably grotesque exhibition of floral bondage.

In times like these, when the result of one's labour falls so far short of expectations, it's useful to focus not on product but on process. That means making the work itself more gratifying, more fun. Here again the wisdom of the elders is invaluable. I remember interviewing a pair of spry old organic growers a few years ago. Running a spread that would have defeated many people half their age, these contented septuagenarians emphasized the importance of making work painless. "People who insist on crawling all day long to weed the carrots—well, they don't have to!" they told me. "You have to have an alternative movement. As you get older, you can't do one thing for four solid hours without a break—and I don't mean a coffee break! You can move firewood and pick some peaches, then weed the tomatoes and then go do some more work."

Spoken like a true workaholic. And it's exactly the advice I receive from my chiropractor when, every spring without fail and some autumns too, I hobble into his office with lower back spasms from too vigorous digging. His suggestions are always wise, and patiently repeated year after year, in the full knowledge that all will be forgotten or ignored. It makes perfect sense that, before starting work, one should loosen up with some stretching exercises, particularly in cool weather. Never lift excessive weights, such as the massive root balls and boulders I regularly trundle around. Lift with your knees and keep your back straight. Use long-handled tools to minimize bending. Switch sides frequently while raking or spading. Stretch and relax in the middle of very vigorous jobs. Sound advice every bit of it, and always remembered with absolute clarity a few moments after a vertebra pops out in protest.

I enjoy strenuous work. Spading the beds in spring and fall is one of the natural year's most marvellous rituals. I love the clean insertion of the spade into loam, the rich scent of fresh-turned earth, the wriggling of upturned worms. I like to pause after a half-hour or so, lean on the spade like Edwin Markham's *The Man with the Hoe*, contemplating the fellowship of earthworkers since time immemorial. At this point in my life it's inconceivable to consider brutalizing this observance with a noisy and polluting rototiller. I think of leaf blowers with scorching sarcasm.

But as musculature and skeleton begin to suffer from accumulated wear and tear, even robust gardeners can fall prey to the seductions of labour-saving devices. Various little scooters and kneeler stools promise the weeder permanent relief from wet, cold, dirty, and stiff knees. Spurious seed dispensers guarantee that you can sow even the tiniest seeds with such precision that the need for thinning is virtually eliminated. Ha! You've got your long-spouted English watering cans so that you never have to stoop to water, and your pneumatic-tired garden carts that will traverse soft earth or rough terrain in a way that no old wheelbarrow ever could. Real dreamers can even get an "organizer belt," a multi-pocket apron with holsters for trowels and forks, a string-dispensing pocket, and pockets for hand pruners, scissors, gloves, and seed packets. I suppose the real advantage here is that you could lose all your tools in one fell swoop, rather than gradually scattering them as you work your way around the garden. I'm not sure if I could ever adapt to the string-dispensing pocket; I've grown so accustomed to having a rat's nest of infuriatingly tangled twine in my pocket, to the challenge of holding up a wayward plant with one hand while trying to untangle twine with the other hand and my teeth.

I know that there are some gardeners among us who really are efficiency experts, those annoying people whose forks and rakes are always hanging on their designated hooks in an immaculate garden shed strategically located within a perfect garden. No matter what time of day you see them, they and their clothes are spotless; it's impossible to catch them smeared with dirt and perspiration the way most of us are when gardening. They seem to float about their estates in stylish attire, snipping a deadhead here, perhaps clipping a wayward shoot over there, humming Mozart as they go. I'm convinced that there's something terribly wrong with these people. I suspect them of hiding some awful secret that will be revealed in due course, leaving flabbergasted neighbours shaking their heads and saying, "I can't believe it; they seemed like such nice people." For myself, and, I think, for most gardeners, fate has decreed a different kind of ignominy. Nothing typifies it better than my great asparagus fiasco.

"Two companionable people who have assembled their materials," writes Eleanor Perényi, "can prepare an asparagus bed in a long springtime afternoon, and enjoy it for years without much additional effort." What could be more tempting, the neophyte wonders, than the prospect of succulent asparagus spears erupting from the earth in early spring, snipped fresh and steamed for no more than a heartbeat? So rich a reward for a simple afternoon's work? And to be repeated year after year: a good asparagus bed is said to produce bumper crops for fifty years or more. It seemed too good to be true. And it was.

I did all the right things. I dug trenches forty centimetres wide and sixty deep. Encountering a couple of enormous boulders in the bed and the stubborn remnant of a tough old fir stump soon extended the job well beyond one springtime afternoon. I heaved heaps of rock and rubble out of the trenches and sifted out the smaller stones. I poured in barrowloads of precious compost and added generous amounts of ground limestone and wood ash. My father shipped out a box of top-notch crowns, sprawled like fleshy white octopi in their peat. Tenderly I set them in their trenches at the prescribed depth of twenty-five centimetres, sixty centimetres apart, and covered them lovingly.

The following spring, wonderful purplish-green spears thrust their soft erotic tips out of the earth. We resisted the urge to harvest any: leave them alone for two years, advised our manual, so they can get established. Again the following year we disciplined the urge to indulge. But the third year's crop was ours to enjoy and what a sublime feast it made! Asparagus, we realized, was one of those crops not worth eating unless cut and rushed immediately to a waiting pot. We cropped it lightly to let the plants grow stronger still. But by the following year, they were looking decidedly unhappy, almost emaciated. We ate very few spears. More compost! More well-rotted manure! But to no avail. By the next spring the few remaining plants lacked all vitality. Their dyspeptic tips could scarcely be called spears at all. Digging down, I found the roots flaccid and defeated.

Two potential causes presented themselves: we discovered that you're supposed to eliminate all female plants, the ones that bear bright berries in the fall, to prevent the bed being colonized by weak offspring. I think by now our bed housed only females and their offspring, like a washed-up patriarch's nightmare of feminist triumph. Furthermore, we learned that it's now recommended that the crowns be planted only a few centimetres below the surface; the old deep-planting regime was for blanching the spears and is currently in disfavour. Oh well, only five years wasted.

I started over again. I ripped out the old crowns, restocked the trenches with new amplitudes of compost, and planted fresh crowns at the newly prescribed depth. In fall we banished all the females with the zeal of real misogynists. But once again we were dragged through the disheartening cycle of a promising first year and thereafter a dismaying falling away to eventual failure.

I talked it over with the locals. A few show-offs do manage to produce bumper asparagus crops year after year, but most had experienced the same melancholy results as myself. Some took their failure quite badly, and there was opportunity here to form an asparagus support group. Instead I opted for that time-honoured alibi for planting failure: I blamed the plants. "Asparagus just doesn't want to grow here," I reasoned, and other failed asparagus farmers were quick to grunt agreement.

For the true workaholic it's galling enough to have an excuse for failure exposed as rot, and twice as bad to see something accomplished casually that you were unable to achieve through unflagging effort. Just off the northern tip of our little island lies an even smaller isle named

Sandy Island. As the name implies, it is formed almost entirely of sand. A fabulous crop of wild asparagus grows there. A crop to make Euell Gibbons drool. Asparagus that flourishes year after year without benefit of trenching, manuring, liming, or irrigation. Nobody prevents the females from seeding. Nobody does anything; the stuff simply grows there in the sand. A more sensitive soul might see in this a cruel mockery of all one's ambitions, all that one has worked for. I choose not to. After ten years of hard labour and disappointment, I just don't think about asparagus any more. Ever.

Planning

$\mathcal{A}$fter several years of milling and haul-
ing, hammering and sawing, our little hand-built home
was more or less completed (amateur owner-builders
soon learn that the job never ends). The house sat,
ungainly and alone, on a large, blank patch of bare earth,
and the question naturally arose: what now? What will
we do with the grounds? To us the expanse of churned
dirt around the house represented just that much more
heavy work ahead. Not yet entirely under the spell of
gardening, we didn't recognize the gift that we'd been
given. For here lay an opportunity that many gardeners
would sell their souls for: the chance to design and create
from scratch a large garden of one's own imagining. A
place to dream crazy dreams and make them real, expe-

rience the sublime storm of genius, learn from nature to discern the very soul of things, see relationships of colour, texture, and form where lesser talents might see none; to create, in short, an ideal of such effortless simplicity yet such elegant common sense as to astound and charm all who beheld it.

Following hard upon house building, with all its bearing weights and stress factors and finicky precisions, the planting of a garden promised to demand little more than good-natured rustic simplicity. The plain matter of deciding what plants to plant where held few intimidations, certainly nothing to rival the acute paranoias construction miscalculations can induce. Not to mention relationship strains. The joint planning and construction of a home is frequently cited as one of the events most certain to generate severe stress, if not outright fracture lines, in a relationship. Some pundits rate it more stressful than infidelity or financial disaster. But, having survived the creation of both house and garden, I think for an amateur team they're equally demanding of mutual tolerance, respect, patience, and transcendental tongue-biting. Designing a garden is a little like having babies: people do it every day. A zillion books and magazines will tell you how. Television and radio shows clog the airwaves with advice. Knowledgeable experts sit by their phones day and night awaiting your call. And yet, like giving birth, the competent creation of a garden can be for the novice a sounding of one's very soul.

Make no mistake, it's far less traumatic and problematic to acquire somebody else's garden and then tinker with it. Any resulting aesthetic shortfalls can be attributed to your predecessors. Where a garden must be started from scratch, smart money has professionals do the job. Should they make a botch of it, you can carp and cavil about them through the next decade of bridge parties. If, on the other hand, things turn out splendidly, you can say it was all your idea and so-and-so simply executed your conceptions. But unless you're impervious to marital friction, as well as to the distinct possibility of exposing yourself publicly as a nincompoop, it's best to stay well clear of garden design.

However, gardeners, like fools, rush in wherever the opportunity presents itself, and there's no point in trying to dissuade them. Greenhorns who'd never dream of trying to play a violin in front of crowds of strangers, who'd squirm with embarrassment if asked to paint a landscape in oils for public viewing, are unfazed by the challenges of designing a garden, which is at least as demanding an assignment as the other two. Because so many of us do it, gardening enjoys the freedoms of folk art. We may not fully understand the finer points of garden design theory, but we know what we like! We read a few books on the subject, perhaps subscribe to a gardening magazine or two, and what more does anyone need?

But then it comes time to decide how the pathways should be laid out, where precisely the shrubbery should go, how long to make the perennial border, what trees need planting where. Each small choice, you realize with a twitch of apprehension, seems contingent upon a dozen others; change one and they all change, like a Rubik's Cube. Planting options tangle together and spiral outwards into a galaxy of really Big Questions. What's the overall vision here, the leitmotif of this garden? What would you say is the underlying principle of the entire composition? Do you intend to work in the organicist or impressionist style? The questions gather around, cocktail glasses in hand, leering at you, inquiring, probing, waiting for you to hesitate or stumble. You begin to suspect that in the matter of garden design enthusiasm may be a less reliable guide than experience. In fact, you feel as if you're taking your first terrifying step out along a fallen log spanning a bottomless chasm.

Never mind. Stick to your game plan. With a thorough understanding of the advantages and limitations of your site and climate, you're well positioned to define your gardening objectives. Unfortunately, this is a step many gardeners postpone until much later in the process, by which time a hodgepodge of random experiments has more or less coalesced into what could be charitably called a vision. This is the rear-view-mirror approach to garden design. Its particular genius flows from what has been called bright-idea planning. "I know," exclaims one of its practitioners, "let's plant some yews!" The very thought of yew is new. But an acquaintance has spoken of them glowingly; or a recent magazine article declared that no worthy garden is ever without a yew; or, most virulent of all, the local nursery has a cut-rate special on yews this week. What could be more appropriate, what could better provide bold vertical strokes? So in go a couple of yews and the bright-idea gardener, enormously pleased, awaits the next lightning bolt of inspiration.

Repeated over time, these ad hoc experiments typically unite within the garden to produce a panorama of daunting gaudiness. Such displays are often described, sometimes enthusiastically, as "a riot of colour." Their ambience is insurrectional. British writer Anne Scott-James identifies five specific gardening styles current in Britain: the suburban style, the working-class style, the Victorian style, the modern town style, and the new cottage style. I would argue that the unplanned pastiches of bright-idea gardeners deserve to be recognized as a style unto themselves. Perhaps it could be called something like the spontaneous gothic gauche style.

For those who don't want their gardens to flounder in chaotic intensity, there's no escaping the chore of defining one's garden objectives. Wise garden writers are indispensable here, serving up nostrums against which only a willful fool would argue. Thus we're encouraged to plan carefully for "a balanced sculptural composition," born of "a dynamic harmony of colours, shapes, textures and structures," resulting in "the creation of aesthetically pleasing arrangements of plants." We achieve these objectives by strict adherence to accepted design principles. "Underlying all the greatest gardens," writes Sylvia Crowe in her classic, *Garden Design*, "are certain principles of composition which remain unchanged because they are rooted in the natural laws of the universe." This is precisely the kind of firm horticultural grounding one is after. But then, just as things are beginning to settle, the writers throw everything overboard in a fit of subjectivism. Even as sensible a gardening author as Louise Beebe Wilder asserts that "each of us should feel free to express himself—his most extravagant, whimsical, ardent, honest self; to work out his own theories and bring his bit of earth to what seems to him its finest and fittest expression." That sounds like yews to me.

Encouraged to pursue extravagance and whimsicality, the gardener is released from the bounds of common sense. So a workaday rule such as "think before you act" is left at the garden gate. Projects, such as the introduction of yews or the wholesale removal of hyperthyroid *Hypericum*, can be initiated on a moment's notice and with infinitely less thought than you'd apply to deciding what dress to wear for dinner.

Whimsicality brushes aside any suggestion that the gardener might benefit from a bit of research. At our place, typically, we laid out and planted quite extensive gardens as an opening gambit, and subsequently became so fascinated with gardening, we began devouring all sorts of written material on the topic. Wonderful surprises awaited us: the adorable little 'Debutante' camellia snuggled so comfortably in a niche by our front door is destined to eventually grow larger than the house and permanently block all hope of entry or exit; the English ivy planted below a north-facing wall we learned was legendary for its house-destroying prowess. The more we discovered, the more complicated the topic became. Doubts and uncertainties began to gnaw like mice in the attic. The only good point to be made for gardening first and researching later is that if we'd done the reading first we might have been sufficiently intimidated to never begin at all. Gardening, like life, is mostly a matter of experience. The best approach, many gardeners conclude, is to leave the heavy research to botanists and hybridizers, instead take tools firmly in hand, and just get out there and do it!

Master gardeners, by comparison, sagely advise the beginner to first carefully examine the possibilities of the site and the expectations that you as a gardener have. How much work are you prepared to do, how much money to spend? Look at the garden and at yourself calmly and dispassionately, and frame the question: what is workable, reasonable, and desirable here? Having made these fundamental landform and lifestyle choices, you would sit at your desk, take out a sheaf of graph paper, and begin a meticulous site plan detailing all the features of the grounds in scale. You'd design your overall garden scheme with specific use areas, access points, and pathways. Eventually you'd design a planting scheme for each bed, where appropriate, to ensure a successive sequence of perfect visual pictures throughout the seasons. You would have wonderfully intense drifts of colour, but never so much as to clash unduly against the garden's *zeitgeist* of calm and tranquility. Your plantings might be of marvellous sumptuousness, but never giddy, never the least bit frivolous. Carefully planned voluptuousness would never descend to indelicacy. Nothing would jangle; nothing would bore; nothing confuse.

This triumph of good taste would largely derive from your adherence to the classic principles of garden design, having to do with concepts such as unity and coherence, scale and balance. The universal laws of proportion would have played a prominent role in your thinking. But there's usually at least one passionate young primitivist in the group prepared to argue that we must smash the old forms and give the high priests of landscape design the bum's rush. The best gardens historically were not consciously designed according to abstract principles, this hothead will insist, but rather evolved organically through the native skills and instincts of generations of good gardeners. We don't need formally planned showcase gardens so much as we need gardens of passionate attachment to Mother Earth. Be bold, this firebrand will urge us, avoid doubts, follow your instincts, plant by the moon, talk to your plants!

You're just about to agree wholeheartedly with this invigorating point of view when, at the other end of the table, the master gardener takes a sip of mineral water, dabs lips with napkin, and fixes everyone with a benign smile. Primitive gardens, the master explains, enjoyed a beauty born from singularity of purpose and nurtured on a strictly limited range of plant materials. Gardeners didn't have exotic species from all over the globe to choose from. Their gardens quite naturally evolved a character perfectly consistent with their site. They could do little else, since their margins of error were blessedly narrow. But today (and here another benevolent smile) neither life nor gardening is as uncomplicated an affair. Our desires, our ambitions, the resources at our disposal have far outstripped the disciplines of a simpler time. In a welter of possibilities, we need to work according to a conscious and deliberate design if we aren't to end up with a dog's breakfast.

Those who argue the need for classic design principles promote none more strenuously than the principle of unity. Unity, they insist, bestows upon the garden a strength of purpose, a continuity with its site and a congruousness of shapes, colours, and textures. Unity permits richness of design within a profound simplicity. Unity forbids a bark mulch pathway leading up to a classic Greek portico. It will not under any circumstances tolerate pink flamingoes within a parterre. Without unity, everything is discord, chaos, confusion.

We know that congruity in plants and materials is an absolute must, but most of us can no more discipline ourselves in plant acquisition than we can stick to our diets. Suppose we've been working along quite nicely in the style of the English cottage garden. Then, by some quirky circumstance we're introduced to a highly attractive haiku poet. We find ourselves newly entranced with things Japanese. The infatuation might start innocently enough with some bamboo wind chimes on the porch, but before you know it, there are miniature Shinto shrines popping up in front of the hollyhocks, and you're tempted to host a tea ceremony among your hostas. Like puppies and small children, multiculturalism is an admirable thing, but not necessarily within the garden.

Travel can be particularly insidious in fomenting disunity. You return from a camping trip in the Sonoran desert with a trunkload of coloured rocks and a newfound passion for desert plantings. After cycling through Holland you simply must have massed tulips at any cost. Rome convinces you that you can no longer live contentedly without a fountain. Once it has a toehold, incongruity has a way of advancing systematically through the garden like quackgrass. The seductions of variety, like ill-considered love affairs, offer a stimulating diversion, an excitement not to be had in the safe and sober inevitability of tastefully selected plants placed in subtly repeated patterns. Gradually one develops into the gardening equivalent of those eminent older men who throw over a lifetime's achievement and run to riotous public debauchery.

Eventually, inevitably, the gardener surveys all that has been brought to fruition and recognizes that there are some real problems here. Perhaps that menacing thick stick of a devil's club wasn't such a great idea after all. Maybe that little clump of mugho pines, hastily parachuted in several years ago to provide "structure," now resembles a depressing huddle of mourners at a pauper's funeral. Sandy and I arrive at this turning point a dozen or more times a year as each successive "show," like a soap-opera star attempting Shakespeare, reveals its limitations. "We need to do some planning," Sandy will announce. Of course we do, but what's most aggravating about these planning sessions is that they confront us squarely with the immensity of our ignorance. Sometimes, shamelessly, I try to sabotage the expedition with sudden outpourings of enthusiasm for some particular small triumph—perhaps a cunning interplay of orange yellows involving the new foliage of a golden spiraea played against the yellow blooms of a pincushion euphorbia and a drift of Rembrandt tulips, their yellow cups streaked with flashes of burnt orange—but the gambit seldom succeeds. There's serious planning work to be done and no nonsense. The point, as Henry Mitchell puts it, rather annoyingly, "is not to dodge complexity but to master it."

We might as well be urged to master the complexities of molecular biology. Design experts flutter about, encouraging us to evoke, in Sylvia Crowe's words, "the compelling force of a central interest played against the seduction of diversion." Right. Meanwhile, we've got our hands full just trying to get the colours figured out. In the much discussed subject of floral colour, several immutable laws work against us. Primary among them is that the flower colour promised in the nursery catalogue, or even in the respectable reference book, is not necessarily the colour you eventually gct. The promised "soft pink" all too often emerges more cloying than cotton candy, and an anticipated "rose madder" might bloom an explosive, fiery orange.

A corollary to this axiom dictates that the more vulgar the colour eventually produced, the longer the plant will take to produce it. We've internalized this little lesson courtesy of several rhododendrons which seemed to require decades of slow but determined growth before producing a bloom. Eventually, of course, they erupted with a shrieking neon iridescence that humiliated every other plant in sight. The consequences of this long delay in showing their true colours are several: the opportunity of returning the offending specimen to whatever reliable source sold it to you in the first place has been irretrievably lost, and once the gaudy misfit has been yanked out, it leaves in its place that much larger a gaping hole in the overall composition.

Here's another colour axiom all gardeners are familiar with: the less desirable the colour, the more durable the plant. The aforementioned fluorescent rhodos were unceremoniously banished from our gardens and, in lieu of incineration, replanted in wild lands outside the fences, where we fully expected them to succumb to the combined depredations of foraging deer, sumo-sized slugs, and summer drought. Needless to say, they've flourished. Meanwhile, the more daintily coloured specimens with which we replaced them have pouted and sulked and been assailed with innumerable ailments.

Even with the most painstaking planning, colour

clashes can erupt in the garden quicker than schoolyard squabbles. We hatched a clever plan one fall to plant a crescent drift of brilliant red tulips behind each of several herbaceous peonies in a mixed border. The vibrant red of the tulips, so the theory went, would play beautifully against the amber stalks of the emerging peonies and, later on, the full peony foliage would mask the unsightly leftover leaves of the tulips. The following spring all unfolded as planned and we congratulated ourselves on the aptness of this cunning little colour combo. Unfortunately, a day or two later, on the terraced bed immediately behind, a large clump of bergenia exploded into bloom, and the contrast of its purplish-pink flowers against the blazing red tulips was such an optical indecency we had to avert our eyes when walking past. Mastering complexity involves seeing the Big Picture.

Bedevilled by colour clashes, smart gardeners fall back on soft grey and silver foliage plants. These are the backroom mediators and conflict-resolution facilitators in the garden. Silvers and greys offer a tone of moderation and coalescence which can draw a tumult of materials and colours into harmonious relationship. Alerted to the potential for serious clashes within our eclectic colour schemes, we planted greys with a vengeance—snow-in-summer and santolina, dusty miller and Arabian thistle, wormwood, mullein, and lamb's ears. Only later did we realize that many of these grey moderators, like grey-faced men in office towers, have a hidden agenda: to take over the earth. Little snow-in-summer—so dainty, so delightful in its Maytime carpet of tiny white flowers— is in reality an insidious ground gobbler. We have an artemisia 'Silver King' that knows no boundaries to its kingdom. Lovely little lamb's ears breed like rabbits, and the great Arabian thistles tower nearly three metres tall with huge pointed leaves sharp as scimitars. Some mornings, especially as the June garden fades, we peek outside and there seems to be nothing but grey visible in any direction, an unrelieved sea of grey, grave and sombre, upon which a few small spots of colour bob like flotsam on a vast expanse of leaden ocean.

But neither a surfeit of grey nor the disunity it seeks to quell are the worst of it. Far worse are what gardeners know as The Gaps. These strange phenomena exist in a space/time warp, appearing in gardens overnight like those mysterious circles found in grain fields. One day a particular planting scheme will be everything it should be: the proportions and forms are perfect, the background plants marvellous in providing textures against which the foreground comes alive, the clever play of colours subtle enough to make Monet drop his palette in amazement. You're enormously pleased with yourself for having pulled it off. Then, just as you're thinking of having a few friends over to behold this tour de force, The Gaps strike. Overnight a great gaping hole opens up in the middle of everything; the entire composition falls hopelessly apart.

The Gaps employ no end of tricks in advancing their subversions. The sudden and unexplained death of a plant central to the scheme is a favourite ploy. Daphnes, of course, are notorious for this, but in our experience, magnolias have been very effective too. You spend years working up a springtime underplanting beneath a star magnolia. When the spring finally arrives in which all your underplanted tulips, daffodils, and anemones, your aubrietias and *Arabis* manifest in full and vibrant glory, you realize that the magnolia has not survived the winter and now looms over the assembled beauty like a cadaverous hanging tree.

A closely related phenomenon involves having an arrangement of several different plants which are supposed to bloom simultaneously, but don't. Instead one is left with some of the plants blooming beautifully and drawing everyone's attention to an area where the neighbouring plants have already finished blooming and are now in a post-bloom funk of deadheads and unsightly foliage that would be better passed over entirely. To confound matters further, we've found that different weather patterns in consecutive years will stimulate growth and blooming differently in various plants: an unusually warm spring may see one plant flowering three weeks ahead of schedule while another genus nearby will scarcely alter its schedule at all.

No such uncertainty stains the reputation oriental poppies have for creating gaps. We have two large clumps of these boisterous characters in different parts of the garden, living like noisy renters under permanent threat of eviction. One clump has flowers of traditional blazing vermilion, the other a less exuberant and more subtle pastel pink salmon colour. Both are splendid in full bloom; massed together, their absurdly large flowers splash a flamboyant rouge across everything that's timid and conservative. "This is life!" these mad revellers cry out, "Be bold! Be wild! For all too soon you die."

I for one am not interested in tiptoeing prudently through life without an annual visit from these reckless libertines. But at what cost! A love affair with oriental poppies ends badly, always. Unable to long sustain such magnificent passion, they collapse. Too soon, far too soon, they're gone, their youthful beauty spent, their tired coarse foliage withered and threadbare. Once fled, oriental poppies leave gaps that loom larger than the national debt.

Then we scurry about, trying to fill in, trying to disguise. We've ringed oriental poppies with daylilies to almost passable effect; we've planted walls of Michaelmas daisies and 'Autumn Joy' sedums in front of them; we've tried baby's breath behind, pulling its frothy veils forward over the sad remnant mounds of departed poppies; we've tried raising whole colonies of cosmos in the greenhouse and transplanting them out mere moments after the poppy foliage is cut down. None of these stratagems is entirely satisfactory. Next year's experiment involves training summer-flowering clematis on curved branches forming a dome over the poppy bed.

Ultimately, the poppy gap may be a cleft in one's heart, inflicted by the loss of youth and beauty, that will never completely heal over. One begins to regret the flirtation with poppies, to reflect upon its foolhardiness. And yet, to think of the following spring without them, to foreswear forever their wild bewitchery ...No, never!

Summer wears on, cicadas sing desultorily and tree frogs croak their patient song for rain. Now, amid the dust and drought, The Gaps approach their moment of apotheosis. Throughout the garden a dull lassitude, a dispiriting torpor, besets so much of what not long before seemed vibrant and fulsome. By the dog days of August the mixed border resembles a fraternity house lounge on Sunday morning. Bare patches leer rudely. Around this time you recall that bit of advice about never planting in focal points or places of high visibility any specimens that have a brief blooming period followed by an eternity of undistinguished foliage. But there they are, nevertheless: prominently placed irises that appear to have malignant melanomas, shrubby *Potentillas* that mistake themselves for tumbling tumbleweeds, summer phlox suffering from dropsy. Most of the day is now spent plumping up Lilliputian annuals in a forlorn hope that they'll fill the gaps and distract the eye from conspicuous lumps of nondescript foliage.

Perversely, in the sultry evenings of summer, new enthusiasms can take root in the gardener's imagination, attractions for plants that beguile with promises of late summer effulgence. That's how hydrangeas worked their way into our place. There was a time not long ago when one wouldn't have been caught dead cultivating a hydrangea, epitomized as they seemed to be by the standard-issue suburban specimens with electric blue heads bigger than basketballs. But times have changed. Nowadays, lacecap hydrangeas particularly are all the rage again, and the unarguable beauty of garden hydrangeas in dried flower arrangements has done wonders to rehabilitate this former outcast. What's most appealing about hydrangeas is that many of them sustain their full glory late in the season when so much else is shrivelled and wizened. They take almost no caring for at all and, wonderful to realize, they're virtually idiot-proof to propagate through softwood cuttings. Say no more! We've spent many a summer evening surreptitiously snipping slips from marvellous old specimens along darkened city boulevards. Up in the cutting beds there now grow lustily enough hydrangeas of all sorts—lacecaps and peegees, big leaf and climbing hydrangeas—to perhaps, just perhaps, banish The Gaps forever. We've put our faith in hydrangeas, along with summer-flowering clematis, the way some people believe the facile promises of electioneering politicians.

I was meandering around the garden one late July morning not long after sunrise. For several weeks the weather had been scorching hot and the earth seemed almost seared. Under my bare feet the pathway stones felt warm and dusty dry. A few melancholy delphiniums hung on still; the monkshood looked to be having a dark night of the soul; chronic fatigue syndrome seemed to grip the remaining old roses. I paused at the bottom of a flight of flagstone steps. Near the top of this wide stairway a cluster of white muskmallows was blooming brilliantly, lit up like candles by a slanting shaft of sunlight. On the next level down, emerging from gaps between the flagstones, grew a crew-cut cluster of feverfew, its compact, lime-yellow leaves and single white daisy-like flowers a vision of freshness and vitality. Another step down, a white and yellow splash of ox-eye daisies completed the setting. All three of them were volunteers, opportunistic self-seeders happy to adapt to Spartan conditions. All are considered coarse and unrefined, meadow weeds really, even though feverfew was once a particular favourite in Victorian gardens. Nobody had planned their appearance here on the steps. Nowhere was this little nomadic trio delineated in a planting scheme on graph paper. There had been no prior discussion about the aesthetic of their asymmetrical triangle, reflecting from the art of Japanese flower arranging the trinity of earth, humans, and heaven. And yet here they were, elegantly descending the stone steps, forming a perfect small arrangement of fresh green foliage and cool, demure whiteness of bloom.

It's a sobering realization that a fair bit of what passes for clever planning at our place is more the result of the lunchbucket work of dependable volunteers and happy accidents. In spring more than a few of our self-celebrated plantings are rescued from dull contrivance and made brilliant by the spreading foam of clear blue forget-me-nots, their countless tiny yellow-eyed flowers brushing the garden with a hazy, lovely wash of blue. Or there will be singular incidents, such as last spring when three spears of a pure white volunteer foxglove perfectly intersected the white flowered dome of a 'Mme. Hardy' rose. No designer could have done it better.

In June, when delphiniums and larkspur lift their flowering towers together, massed common foxgloves, volunteers all, stand boldly erect in the background, their blooming spires well over two metres tall, heavy with pendulous flowers—creamy whites and purples, pinks and mauves freckled with magical small runes. They are a perfect blue-collar counterpart to the aristocratic refinements of delphiniums. Together they raise their colourful arms skywards in a massed egalitarian choir of praise.

In the full sun of summer, volunteer poppies pop up all over the place, equally indifferent to soil conditions, weather, and whatever clever planting schemes we may have envisaged. Iceland, Shirley, and opium poppies sow themselves in brave little colonies and wave their brilliant pastel papery flowers like the multicoloured flags of assembled nations.

At our place there's no happier naturalizer than the California poppy. A perennial that behaves like an annual in our climate, it sows itself with astounding profligacy. By late summer they're everywhere, covering dry banks and awkward corners with their ferny blue-green foliage and masses of satiny flowers, coloured from pale yellow to rich custard gold. You can't get much closer to paradise than to walk through whole meadows of these blooming beauties along the sea cliffs of Oregon and northern California, with the Pacific surf thundering far below.

The magic of the gardens I like best seems a combination of happy accidents, lusty volunteers, and the bold experiments of adventuresome gardeners. There's an easy blowziness, a natural nonchalance about these places. The plants seem clustered together for their own enjoyment, in combinations that flatter each plant, its immediate neighbours and the garden as a whole. The casual correctness of these magic places is, of course, illusory. Over time they've no doubt seen more trial and error than a circuit court. Their gardeners are themselves strange hybrids: part artists, part technicians, part graduates of the "wait and see" school of landscape design. When something doesn't work, out it goes and in goes something else. And when it does work, when everything falls into place and the best-laid plans come to fruition with a carefree precision, an impeccable grace and correctness, then the gardener stands easy for a moment and all's right with the world.

8

Trees

*W*e cinched a chain around the sturdy trunk of the tree, hooked the chain to the rear end of a half-ton, and hit the gas. Tires spun wildly, spitting gravel. The chain stretched taut. Stubbornly, the tree held its ground. We hit the gas again, and roots began popping loose underground. Straining against the chain, the tree began to list like an overmatched arm wrestler. More roots popped and split, and in a final paroxysm, the tree released its grip on the earth and fell. Dragged rudely across the ground, stripped of branches, its roots torn and mangled, the poor thing looked like a goner. "I think it'll be fine," said Jack.

A retired schoolteacher, our neighbour Jack was one of those enigmatic characters who always look on the bright side of life while wearing a habitual frown. He'd invited us over to his place to try salvaging a sugar plum tree he no longer wanted. By the look of it, the tree was at least thirty years old, maybe four metres high, heavily and badly pruned in the past, with a trunk about twenty-five centimetres thick. To me it seemed a little large for our amateur transplant team, but Jack was all optimism. Under his supervision, we'd dug around the drip-line, excavating a huge rootball and severing any far-reaching roots with mattock blows. We tried to lever the rootball out with steel pry bars, but roots still intact underneath wouldn't let go. That's when Jack hit upon the half-ton haul-out technique. While it accomplished his objective—to get rid of the tree—this violent extraction seemed to have defeated ours, which was to acquire a living fruit tree with branches and roots, not a mutilated corpse.

Replanted back at the homestead, flagship of our future orchard, the thing looked more like a warped Edwardian hatrack than a tree. Only three small green-wood branches remained attached to a knot of truncated limbs. But, lo and behold, the following spring all three leafed out, the way legends tell of leaves sprouting from the walking sticks of saints. Miraculous new shoots appeared. Within two years the sad-sack stump had developed an entire crown of branches and was beginning to resemble a tree again. Today, twenty years later, it's a vigorous big tree that fills our summers with baskets of juicy sweet sugar plums. Damned if old Jack wasn't right all along!

The case of the death-defying sugar plum formed our

introduction to that venerable tradition among gardeners of digging up massive chunks of living flora and
moving them to someplace, anyplace, else. As well, the
experience proved an eloquent lesson in the mystifying
unpredictability of trees. All too often, the exercise
foreshadowed, a tree which should die doesn't, and one
that shouldn't die does. Trees, we were to learn, have
predilections of their own. One of the most magnificent
components of gardening, trees also offer the amateur
grower the grandest opportunities for blundering on a
colossal scale. Choosing the wrong species, locating it
improperly, planting it incorrectly, pruning it inappro-
priately—a good-sized tree can easily become a monument to incompetence visible for blocks. Not to mention
becoming a menace: a problem tree can blight your
garden, enrage the neighbours, flatten your house, an-
tagonize authorities, and, ultimately, skewer you on the
horns of ethical dilemma.

The planting of trees is normally born of honourable
intentions. You decide you want a few trees around the
old place. Your rationale is unassailable: North America
has been systematically stripped of her great forests, and
you'd like to do your little bit to reverse this appalling
shortsightedness. As you've often mentioned in your
letters to the editor about the Brazilian rain forest, trees
are the lungs of the planet, breathing in carbon dioxide
and breathing out oxygen: the exact opposite of what we
do. Trees and we are like Inuit throat singers, exchanging

breath back and forth. Trees cool and soothe us, encourage wildlife, and act as carbon sinks. They reconnect us with our ancient arboreal forebears and with the sacred groves in which our ancestors worshipped nature spirits.

Trees, in short, are altogether admirable. So commendable are they, our enthusiasm can subvert common sense. Down at the nursery we're confronted with dozens, perhaps scores, of different kinds, all of which look wonderful. How to choose? The question raises the issue of left- and right-brain thinking. Left brainers will lean towards a rational and logical selection method: thoroughly researching what trees do best in the local environment, what growing conditions they require, how they interact with nearby plantings and structures, what maintenance they need, and, most critically, how large they eventually grow. The only drawback to this system is that too often the selection is based upon bookish descriptions rather than experiencing the tree as a living thing. Right brainers, on the other hand, trust more to instinct and emotion. Their method is to wander the nursery until they encounter a tree that feels right. A certain cut of leaf or texture of bark might appeal, a particular intricacy of branching pattern might intrigue; there'll be something ineffable, something numinous about a certain specimen. On dull days, interesting times can be had in nurseries just watching couples of mixed persuasion hashing out what tree to select.

Size of yard is, of course, a determining factor. Abundance of space, such as we have, amplifies opportunities for both triumph and catastrophe. Over the years we've managed to acquire a dizzying assortment of trees. We've got the inescapable ornamental cherries and plums and crab apples. Our willow collection includes weeping, contorted, and various pussy willows. Of course we had to have a couple of different birches, and at least a few Japanese maples, along with a paperbark maple and a weeping silver pear. Lots of dogwoods, naturally, and a redbud to go with them. A *Davidia* seemed like a good idea at the time. The laburnum and the oaks were given to us. Once we'd gotten the golden honey locust it only seemed right to put a goldenrain tree beside it. Then came the exotic specimens we hadn't planned on but couldn't resist: the silk tree, the ginkgo, the dawn redwoods and plume cryptomeria. There are others, but you get the idea.

Experienced gardeners realize that, with a list like this, a yard runs the risk of resembling a mongrel arboretum splotched with mismatched specimens. Happily, parsimony has saved us, at least for the moment. Operating under strict budgetary restraints, we've seldom gone out and actually bought a large, healthy tree and plopped it in for instant effect. Instead, we've taken the path of gradualism, including growing some trees from seed, a process so slow it would make Job jumpy. We have a lovely little blue spruce from seed, now at least five years old and scarcely over ankle-height. Other trees have come by way of cuttings—the willows being almost excessively co-operative this way. Trees we actually laid out cold cash for tended to be either puny runts in one-gallon pots or sale-priced deviants like the distorted

Japanese cherry we purchased despite its apparent determination to develop as a horizontal shrub. Few of these misfits and foundlings are big enough yet to be visible above nearby shrubs and perennials—some may never be—and thus we've avoided for the moment any potential for clutter or clash. I highly recommend this "small is beautiful" approach to anyone feeling the least bit queasy on tree questions. I'm certain it's how bonsai got started.

No matter if you're dealing with a hundred trees as we are, or with only one, proper placement is critical. The odds against planting a tree in the right place are roughly equivalent to those against winning a multi-million-dollar lottery. As a rule, there is only one completely right location and an infinite number of wrong ones. Again, left brainers will insist upon studying the site for soil and exposure conditions, current and future uses of the space, and the location of buildings, utilities, and existing plants. But there are more adventuresome approaches. Planting tall-growing specimens under power lines, for example, is a popular option that many of us have explored. If layout prevents planting directly under the lines, a good second-best is to place the tree so that its branches will regularly hit the lines during windstorms.

For real daredevils, a big tree looming over the house on a dark and stormy night can generate enough terror to make Stephen King take fright. Not long ago I saw an old catalogue advertising Colorado blue spruce seedlings. An accompanying illustration depicted several prim little specimens planted in a small lawn in front of a ranch-style bungalow. The ad mentioned nothing about these being dwarf varieties. Nor was there any mention that these lovely little Christmas trees would eventually tower thirty or more metres high, creating a monstrous spruce grove straight from an ancient temperate rain forest, plunging home and yard into perpetual shade and threatening to flatten the respectable little rancher if one of them should ever topple over. I know all about this because our small house huddles in the lee of a wall of huge native firs, cedars, and hemlocks. When the south-easters howl, these big conifers rattle and crack and bang their crowns together. Tops and limbs snap off and hurtle to the ground; occasionally a whole tree topples over with an earth-shaking thump! Lying awake during a storm, rigid with terror, I wait for one of the giants to come down and flatten our house. Anyone can add this kind of excitement to their lives by simply getting a huge, shallow-rooted tree growing close to the house on the windward side. Even if the tree doesn't fall over, its branches can batter away at the roof, siding and windows, causing considerable damage while terrorizing the inhabitants.

A less dramatic, more subversive sort of terror network can be had through creative placement of trees with highly invasive roots. Poplars and willows are popular choices. Their voracious root systems can plug sewer pipes, crack basement walls and foundations, and cause sidewalks to heave. Pedestrians tripping over crumpled sidewalks and suing for compensation for broken hips or mental distress can add a certain human interest to the gardener's otherwise botanical routine. Trees that obscure street lights, traffic signs, or approaching vehicles can also achieve the same litigious effect. Speaking of sewer lines, even non-invasive trees can add interest if planted immediately above sewers or other underground utilities which, sooner or later, need to be dug up for repairs. With trees, these provocative developments may not manifest themselves until years later, by which time the planter has often moved on to work similar arboreal wonders elsewhere, leaving new owners, accessories after the fact, to reap the whirlwind.

There's an old proverb that says the best time to plant a tree was twenty years ago. This is how we feel looking at our minimalist collection: if only we'd planted them years ago, how grand they'd be today! The next best time to plant, an addendum to the proverb says, is right now. Several problems present themselves. The first concerns the nature of the planting hole. Most gardening manuals advise digging a wide and deep hole in which to spread the roots, but sharp differences of opinion occur as to how to fill the hole. Traditionalists recommend backfilling with good garden soil bolstered with compost, peat moss, and manure. More recently we're told to skip the amendments, that the critical thing is to get homogeneity in the root zone soil to facilitate uniform water penetration into the total rooting area. Then the old guy down the road tells you it all depends upon whether you're planting a bare-root or container-grown tree. But pretty soon his wife joins the conversation and says she read in a magazine somewhere that you shouldn't be excavating a big hole at all because it just acts as a water trap and drowns the roots.

Before they've finished bickering about it, you've run smack into another problem: should you prune the tree back before planting? "Absolutely," one expert tells you, "you have to get your root/shoot ratio right or you're in trouble. Cut it back hard and give the tree a chance to get established before forcing it to sustain all that top growth." By the time you've located your pruning shears and got back to the tree, somebody else has showed up who tells you not to touch a single twig. A tree's vitality is stored in the branches, you're told, so leave them be. Perplexed, you consult your manual, which tells you that different trees have different requirements, and that the experienced nurseryman from whom you buy your tree will advise you as to whether or not it should be pruned and how. You're not entirely convinced that the high-school students punching cash registers at your nearby franchise nursery qualify as experienced nurserymen.

Eventually you get the tree into the ground, generally at a level either low enough that it'll produce basal sprouting every year for the rest of your life, or high enough to render irrigation impossible. Next you realize that you should probably stake it in order to hold it upright. Driving a thick stake straight through the rootball is arduous work and may succeed in killing the tree. If not, a wire or stout rope wrapped tightly around the trunk and fastened to the stake may induce death by strangulation several years later. Many stakes possess the singular attribute of splitting or rotting just when they're most needed. Not long ago we had a sizable weeping willow crash over into the pond due to a heavy snow load and a well-rotted stake.

Such catastrophes are commonplace with fast-growing characters like willows. What's the old saying?—a willow will buy you a horse before an oak will pay for a saddle. But the slowpokes have charms of their own. We have a tamarisk labouring away on a warm and well-drained hillside where it ought to be perfectly content. After fifteen years it's still smaller than a hollyhock. You begin to wonder if perhaps the tree was rootbound to begin with and you neglected to break open the roots. Then you're faced with a fine choice: leave it alone and hope it corrects the problem itself, or dig it up in a weakened condition and risk killing it. But with trees, everything's relative: the tamarisk towers like a sequoia compared with our silk tree. A native of Asia, *Albizia julibrissin* likes to keep warm, and we are on the furthest fringe of its hardiness. But when you've seen one of these beauties spreading its ferny foliage in soft undulations topped by a foam of frothy pink flowers, you simply must have one. So we do. Sort of. Every year it throws up an ambitious leader about a metre high. Every fall the new growth fails to harden off properly. Every winter it's killed back down to the ground. This has been going on for years, and we've adapted by coming to think of it as more of an anorexic perennial than a tree.

Seasonal die-back on a marginally hardy species is the least of the problems facing an amateur arborist. Far more pressing, for example, is the "Oops, I planted the wrong tree!" syndrome. Symptoms may become evident shortly after planting or may be delayed for many years. Here's an example. Within our eclectic assortment of trees, place of honour in the front garden was accorded to several varieties of ornamental crab apples, both white- and pink-flowering. A splendid choice, you might say, and so they seem in early May when their flower buds are tinged with a pink of exquisite purity, then open to form garlands of gorgeous blossoms strung along branches fresh with new greenery. Gazing into this splendour, one is swept away in imagination to mediaeval festivals where young innocents cavort upon the grass to the music of lutes while the May Queen smiles with ethereal beauty.

Sometime after this dazzling vision was first experienced, we came across the unwelcome information that crab apples, especially in the Pacific Northwest, suffer severe problems with apple scab, rust, powdery mildew, and borers, and that particular care must be taken to plant disease-resistant varieties. In our case, I must admit, particular care was not taken. If memory serves, we obtained our crabs on the spur of the moment at a bargain-basement price from a nursery that had declared bankruptcy.

At such a poignant moment of realization, one is vulnerable to recrimination and self-loathing, and care should be taken to provide a personal safety net. I find that nothing works quite so well as contemplating even grosser blunders committed by other people, the effect being considerably enhanced if the blunderer is somebody who ought to have known better. In the case of our haphazardly selected crabs, I was cheered considerably by reading about Vita Sackville-West's miscalculation with lime trees. Wanting to develop a grand avenue of pleached limes at Sissinghurst, the great lady had her gardeners put in common limes *(Tilia x europaea)*. The trees were a disaster, repeatedly throwing up vigorous suckering basal shoots and attracting hordes of aphids. Eventually, after a half-century of frustration, the National Trust had the whole works torn out and replanted properly. In a context like this, with history itself looking on, a few anonymous little crabs seem like not such a calamity after all.

There are, as well, what are called noxious trees. Several native species out our way get labelled, perhaps unfairly, in this category. One is the bigleaf maple, a "weed tree" that grows at a prodigious rate, prevents most other plants from living under it, seeds prolifically and rains down a steady shower of dead branches and twigs. Needless to say, we have about six big specimens at our place, valued mostly for their thin but wholesome maple syrup in spring and their generous autumn drop of leaves for leaf mould. Some people curse ash and oak trees—both considered sacred in ancient days—because of their prolific seeding. Horse chestnuts and catalpas provoke a lot of squawking about their droppings, and really fastidious people gripe about the messiness of arbutus, paulownia, and dove trees too.

Where the fun really starts, however, is in having a problem tree that impacts upon neighbouring properties. I remember a case involving a magnificent weeping willow growing near the back lot line of a suburban house not far from us. Its owners prized the tree for its grace and beauty as well as the privacy it afforded by screening the house and yard abutting the rear of their lot. Unfortunately, the residents of this adjoining lot were avid gardeners. Situated due south of them, the big willow cast most of their growing area into deep shade, and the tree's invasive roots sucked both moisture and nutrients out of their garden soil. The situation entailed lengthy negotiations, eventual impasse, the breaking-off of negotiations, rude remarks, threats, curses, and eventually the engagement of attorneys. General consternation ran throughout the neighbourhood. Finally the aggrieved gardeners pruned off every branch of the tree that infringed upon their airspace, leaving a grotesquely one-sided willow as a monument to human problem-solving.

Even on your own property, without the interference of neighbours, dealing with a problem tree is sometimes easier said than done. For one thing, municipal regulations may prohibit or limit tree cutting. Consider the case of Paul Levy, a San Francisco lawyer who wanted to cut down a Monterey pine that was undermining his vacation home in that trendiest of seaside towns, Carmel.

The pine's roots were beginning to heave Levy's floor, and its trunk was buckling his bedroom wall. Unfortunately, all this came to a head in 1992, which had been declared Year of the Tree in Carmel. Understandably, authorities took a dim view of Levy's plans. The local forest commissioner said the fault lay not with the pine but the plaintiff, because Levy had knowingly built his addition over the roots twenty years earlier. Quoth the commissioner: "It didn't sneak up on him in the middle of the night."

Short of barging into your bedroom, trees can cause other sorts of mischief. Wind storms bring out the worst in them, especially with large trees that have been damaged by incompetent pruning or careless bulldozer work, or giants that have been weakened by root rot, canker, or crotch cracking. A couple of years ago we experienced a freak winter storm packing wildly gusting northeast winds. Trees were flopping over as indiscriminately as drunken uncles at a wedding. We happened at the time to be staying in a suburb recently carved out of forestland. To enhance property values, the developers had left numbers of large Douglas fir trees scattered throughout the lots. When the freak wind struck, many of these isolated trees came crashing down, several of them right through the fashionably shingled roofs of executive homes. For the next few weeks local "tree surgeons" did a land-boom business amputating every standing tree in sight.

When it comes to tree pruning, the average gardener falls somewhat short of professional arborists, who can scamper up the tallest trees on climbing spurs, expertly saw off enormous limbs, and lower them smoothly down on ropes. Amateur pruners, by comparison, largely fall into one of two categories: indiscriminate hackers or timid tip snippers. The former are wood butchers, deviant personalities eager to perpetrate chainsaw massacre on any available tree. Mutilated stumps and deformed limbs are their legacy. They specialize in "topping" trees, that is, knocking their heads off. The results are aesthetically questionable: at best you get a scalped head silhouetted against the sky. At worst, depending upon tree species, you may get centre rot from the exposed cut, or a rapid resprouting of poorly attached and hazardous branches, or ultimately a very tall dead stump. Topping is the tree surgeon's version of lobotomy.

Most real gardeners, happily, are found at the opposite end of the pruning spectrum, surprisingly diffident, fearful of making too unkind a cut. We snip and clip and nip well enough, but when it comes to truncating or amputating we grow faint, we hesitate to make too bold a stroke for fear we'll mutilate the tree irretrievably.

Nowadays our anxieties are compounded because pruning has become political. Tree preservation societies and tree rights groups with names like Plant Amnesty confront us with their ambition "to end the senseless torture and mutilation of plants." They talk intriguingly about "tree compartments" and "respecting the tree's defense boundaries" by employing the "target pruning method." Topping, they tell us, is an old-fashioned barbarism and no longer done. Rather, a well-pruned tree with strong branch attachments and natural-looking structure is a more attractive, healthier, and safer tree. You're impressed. Unfortunately, this sort of talk also tends to intensify your fear of pruning. Timid to begin with, you become almost catatonic. You spend long hours pondering the political correctness of tip pruning.

How, for example, can I justify the radical surgery I perform each April on several young eucalyptus trees in one of our borders? Like other members of its family, this species has a different leaf in its juvenile and adult stages. As a young tree, the leaves are a delightful silvery-blue and grow as a disc encircling the stem. They're commonly used in dried flower arrangements. If left to mature, however, the tree becomes a scraggly ten-metre-high item with long, dull, and undistinguished leaves. In the border you train it like a shrub, cutting off most of the previous year's growth and leaving a stump about a metre high. Almost immediately, it throws out new shoots, and by midsummer it's once again a gorgeous fountain of arched stems shimmering with silvery leaves. But let's face it: my radical intervention is condemning these plants to a shortened life of extended adolescence, like the Vatican choir boys who were castrated to keep their voices soprano. Even while delighting in the wonderful blue-grey eucalyptus foliage through the depths of winter, I wonder how long this sort of thing can go undetected by the tree rights movement.

But then I reassure myself that even if a pro-eucalyptus faction did show up, they probably wouldn't make it past our orchard. Here we feature an eye-catching display of semi-dwarf apple trees that have been thinned and headed, both winter and summer, for many seasons and now look as though a row of scarecrows had taken up tai chi. Their problems stem from a scarcely adequate supply of sunshine. Encircled by huge native conifers, these valiant little fruit trees stretch their branches skyward, reaching for the sun. My mission, in order to ensure the maximum fruit production obtained from horizontal branches, is to force the growth back down by whatever means are available. Judicious pruning goes a long way. By constantly cutting back to a bud on the underside of each branch, I've succeeded in developing limbs that descend at bizarre angles like the arms of Balinese dancers.

With intractable branches, I go further. I force them down by weighting them with plastic bags of sand. Recommended by one of our radio talk-show gardeners, this technique has its limitations. Too little sand has no effect and the branch carries on with its vertical ascent. Too much, and the branch sags down and eventually tears off. The perfect amount of sand is an impossibility, because it gets heavier in damp weather and lighter in dry. Left too long in sunlight, the bags split open and disgorge their contents, releasing the branches to swing skyward again, with the added adornment of torn plastic bags. The end result is a tree festooned with tattered plastic in various states of decomposition hanging from angular branches, half of which point skyward and the other half earthward. Even a modest-sized orchard of these creations, such as we have, I feel confident is sufficient to repel any tree-rights investigators.

On the other hand, it would be false modesty to imply that there haven't been a few small successes. Five or six years ago we bought a deformed little redbud tree which we planted near the deck for summer shade. Several dogwoods grow nearby, and the idea is that the pink-flowering redbud and white-flowering dogwoods blooming simultaneously will create a show of exquisite beauty. We'll see. Meantime, the misshapen little redbud needed help. I pruned out all the dead, damaged, and distorted growth first. Then off came any crisscrossing branches, or shoots growing back through the centre of the crown. As we've all been told more than enough, there's a correct way to trim branches, neither too close to the limb, nor so far away as to leave a stub. And how many times do we need to hear that, when heading back a branch, be sure to cut diagonally neither too close nor too far from a growth bud? Somehow these refinements are more easily attained when you're not balanced precariously on the top rung of an old stepladder, getting poked in the eye by branches, and wielding pruning shears that were last sharpened during the Boer War.

Today our ungainly little urchin of a redbud has grown into graceful adolescence. Its crown is nicely rounded, its branches finely tiered in horizontal patterns. Last spring, for the first time, it produced small clusters of rosy pink flowers, like miniature sweet peas, along its bare twigs and branches. After flowering, its heart-shaped coppery green leaves unfurl to form a perfect dappled shade. At moments like this the arborist swells with the justifiable pride of accomplishment. Earlier inhibitions are cast aside and more complicated pruning manoeuvres contemplated. You start entertaining fantasies of creating espaliered goblets out of apple trees trained in the French Renaissance style. Perhaps a bit of topiary would give the old place some much-needed structure. You see yourself executing clipped yew peacocks like the ones at Hidcote Manor, or perhaps domes of manicured box lining a long axial path as at Tintinghull House in Somerset. Maybe you'll try your hand at pleached hornbeams. Who knows?

Let me confess openly: I have been having an affair with trees. I hug them unabashedly, caress them affectionately, watch them for hours, follow their seasonal cycles with excitement. I've walked enraptured among the stout old oaks of England, sat on a herb-scented hillside in Greece gazing down at the sublime counterpoint of softly rounded olive trees and slender cypress spires, stood astounded at the massive ancient bulk of red-trunked giant sequoias. I've also, reluctantly, felled big trees, milled them, and built our home from them.

Playwright Thornton Wilder once wrote that "the planting of trees is the least self-centred of all that we do. It is a purer act of faith than the procreation of children." I like that. I like to imagine the purple beech we planted three years ago still growing three hundred years from now, a huge and beautifully spreading specimen admired by all who see it, centuries after all of us are dead and long forgotten. As British garden designer and author Russell Page put it, "To plant trees is to give body and life to one's dream of a better world." So too is the defence of our last great remnant forests. Tree hugging, a common pastime in our part of the world, is not an act of naive romanticism, but a gesture of passionate prudence, born of an instinct for survival and a dream of a better world. Amen.

9

Lawns

When I was a lad and Elvis was king, back in the fifties, mowing the lawn meant just one thing: a blister-raising bout with the dreaded reel lawnmower. Today, only thirty years later, these contraptions look like quaint museum pieces, ancient and hopelessly inadequate. But in our neighbourhood they were state-of-the-art. Sure, a few up-and-coming types had gone off and purchased power mowers; but they were the exception, and not altogether approved of. Most people pushed—or got some gawky kid like myself to do it, for fifty cents per lawn.

At our house we didn't really have a lawn. We'd started out with one: when my dad sent back to England a couple of fuzzy snapshots of the little clapboard house he'd just bought in Toronto to be our new home, my brothers and I thrilled to see that the new family estate included what seemed to us a vast expanse of lawn and three mighty trees. Compared with our working-class row house in Liverpool, this was a veritable wilderness in the wonderful wild country of Canada.

Sure enough, when we arrived at the frontier, the place sprawled like a country acreage. We could actually toss a ball on the front lawn and clamber up into the knobbly cedar trees that lined the narrow lot front. But not for long. My dad chopped the cedars down—"dirty trees" in his opinion—and dug up the scrawny lawn to make a real English garden. The tangled grass and knock-kneed lilac bushes in the backyard went the same way, replaced by trim currant bushes and orderly rows of vegetables. Within a year, every scrap of ground was under intense cultivation, and not a blade of grass remained. In this we were singular. There wasn't a lot on the street, possibly not one in the entire district, that had neither front nor back lawn. Passersby stared at our place as though we were living in a yurt.

Perversely, this embarrassing lack of grass didn't relieve us boys of lawnmowing duty. Deprived of our own lawn, we were sent off to cut the lawns of others for pay; and that meant coming to grips with the redoubtable reel mower. Writer Eleanor Perényi recalls the old reel mowers with nostalgia for "lost summer mornings when one was awakened by the gentle crescendo and diminuendo of their whirring blades, and the perfume of new-mown grass drifted through an open window." All very

nice for those lying abed, I suppose, but for us poor
flunkies out there doing the pushing, the damn thing
seemed the most hellacious contraption ever invented. I
can still feel the blisters on the palms of my hands, still
remember the obstinate tangles of grass in which the
blades would become enmeshed, and still recall trying to
pull out clogging wads of grass without losing a finger.
The machine itself, invented in 1830 by a chap named
Edwin Budding, was not entirely to blame: I suspect
certain of my clients didn't oil the moving parts or
sharpen the blades, ever. And, being careful of their fifty-
cent pieces, perhaps some let the grass grow over-long
between trimmings.

So my heart soared when at last I graduated from this
misery to the snarling roar and belching fumes of a
gasoline-powered mower. The model I lost my innocence on was a gas-driven reel mower, a huge beast of a
thing with a Briggs and Stratton engine perched over an
outsized reel of twirling blades. When you fired it up,
after several dozen pulls on a thick cord, it roared like
Beelzebub and spewed a purple haze for blocks. With
drive-wheel engaged, the thing took off like an enraged
bull at Pamplona, dragging me behind it. This monster
belonged to the parish priest, a surly old tyrant for whom
I slaved on Saturdays. Happily, the scrawny lawns of his
new church yard were planted on excavated subsoil and
resembled the hair on a mangy dog. Sparse and scanty,
the lawns were extensive, but unbroken by trees or other
obstacles. I could fire up Beelzebub and take a straight
run for thirty or forty metres before thumping to a stop
by running into one of the church walls.

I realize that push mowers are enjoying a renaissance of sorts nowadays. People with smallish lawns are gravitating to push mowers because they are environmentally sound, healthy, and altogether praiseworthy. I applaud these people; I want to be numbered among them; but I suspect they never pushed for pay in the early days. I can't help thinking of them as dabblers, the sort of amateurs who were urged to buy Budding's ingenious new invention as "an amusing, useful and healthy exerciser for the country gentleman."

Contemporary lawns are not the playing fields of dilettantes; they are the grounds of a rigorous *realpolitik*. In the world of lawnery, America stands alone as an unchallenged superpower. America has some eighty thousand square kilometres of lawn, enough to cover the entire state of Illinois. About 80 per cent of the total is in private property, the rest in golf courses, playing fields, and parks. Two-thirds of American metropolitan homes are single-family dwellings surrounded by yards. And in America, yards mean lawns. Fifty million home-owners fuss over the lawns of the nation. The lawn turf business alone is worth a whopping 30 billion dollars a year.

Lawns are big business and, let's face it, largely men's business. Perhaps that's a consequence of us legions of teenage boys earning pocket money by mowing, or perhaps the sheer single-mindedness of bare grass appeals to us. Could it be that clipped grass evokes glorious memories of the brilliant diving catches we used to make in centre field, or the time we took a little hitch pass in the flat, shook off the cornerback, and romped eighty yards for a game-winning touchdown? Golf, soccer, frisbee—there's no end of games you can play on grass. Characteristically, we guys have risen to the challenge of providing good grass by bringing on the heavy hardware—thunderous mowers, whining weed-eaters and leaf-blowers, ear-splitting aerators, anything that consumes fuel, spews fumes, and wakes up the neighbours. Womenfolk may be content to quietly crawl around on their hands and knees weeding perennial borders; we'd rather turn the front yard into the Indianapolis Speedway, or mount our huge rider-mowers like grizzled farmers on a combine, off to cut our lower five square metres of grass.

But why? Why this compulsion to swathe the earth with close-clipped greenery? Here's fertile ground indeed for all sorts of philosophers and eco-historians. The Savanna Syndrome hypothesis has had a lot of play. "Encoded in our DNA," explains Michael Pollan in *Second Nature*, "is a preference for an open grassy landscape resembling the shortgrass savannas of Africa on which we evolved." Moving us along from hunter-gatherers to herdspeople, Thorstein Veblen thinks we take delight in lawns because we are a race "whose inherited bent is to readily find pleasure in contemplating a well-preserved pasture or grazing land." Writing in the *Washington Post*, Curt Suplee concludes: "The origins of the lawn are shrouded in the mists of antiquity. Aztecs, Mayans, precolonial American Indians and ancient Persians are variously reported to have gloried in grass; so are the Chinese emperors of the second century B.C."

But it was Europeans, and the English especially, who began lifting the love of grass out of the natural and into the world of abnormal psychology. A German count living in 1260 considered that "the sight is in no way so pleasantly refreshed as by fine and close grass kept short." The *Oxford Dictionary* gives 1548 for the appearance of the noun "lawn." Shakespeare writes of the "grasse-plat," meaning a piece of ground covered with turf, sometimes ornamented with flower beds. A "greenyard" in Elizabethan days was an enclosure covered with grass in which stray animals were impounded or in which hounds took their exercise.

Just how these grasse-plats and greenyards evolved into today's suburban lawn is a matter of conjecture. Various thinkers speculate that the lawn emulates the Tudor bowling alley or the aristocratic deer park or the English village green or the French allée. By 1773, *Oxford* reveals, the definition of lawn had expanded from "a stretch of untilled or grass-covered ground" to include "a portion of a garden etc. covered with grass, which is kept closely mown." The mowing, when not done by grazing animals, was accomplished through repeated scythings, and grand estates employed teams of skilled labourers whose expert scything sheered expansive lawns to uniform smoothness.

Uniquely the product of a damp, cool climate in which bent grasses thrive, the lawn developed into a pardonable fetish for British aristocrats. But in much of

North America, the rationale collapses. The climate is often unsuitable for lawns; the terrain is sometimes impossible for lawns; the soil may be entirely wrong for lawns; the natural plant succession of a region may be inimical to lawns. None of this has been sufficient to deter us. Colonials to the bone, North Americans have spared no effort in aping the landscaped parks of gentrified Britain.

Transplanted to America, the lawn quickly became cluttered with a great confusion of myths and symbols which spoke of attitudes towards class, democracy, morality, and nature. If the first pilgrims to the so-called New World experienced the forested wilderness as a forbidding place, hostile and inhospitable, murderous with savages and ravening beasts, the lawn may have represented a clearing-away of the menace, an open, sunlit area across which no danger might approach unnoticed. Perhaps it also served as a reminder of the "green and pleasant land" the settlers had left behind. Layered over this "man against the wilderness" motif lies American ambivalence about class. Expansive lawns make sense on large properties devoted to leisurely pursuits: the old term "lawn-meet" referred to the gathering of a hunting party, with horses and hounds, in front of an English gentleman's house. From these aristocratic roots we fall heir to a conviction that people of the proper sort simply have lawns. Not to have a lawn—and this my parents failed to grasp in our blue-collar Toronto neighbourhood—denotes a lack of breeding.

In America, breeding ground of crackpot evangelism,

the lawn fetish soon clothed itself in the garment of righteousness. The lawn came to represent salvation. Anthropologist Gloria Levitas is quoted in the *Washington Post* as saying, "The grass tamed represents the wilderness tamed. Keeping it mowed and managed signifies a state of grace—to subdue nature yet live within it." The condition of yards in general, and front lawns in particular, came to signify the moral character of the inhabitants. In 1914, the U.S. Steel Corporation, anxious to elevate the morals of immigrants toiling in its mines and mills to the company's own high ethical standards, issued this advice: "Gardens and beautiful lawns help to make homes. A home means more than mere shelter from the elements. The beauty of the gardens and lawns exert a refining influence on the family, which shows inside the house and in the behaviour of the members of the family towards each other."

Besides keeping its labour force out of saloons and brothels, lawn and garden care, said the company, would get the workers "out into the open air and sunshine. This is especially beneficial to those who work in mines and mills."

Ethics and aesthetics met in the front yard of America and institutionalized the lawn. Landscape architect Frederick Law Olmstead, the chap who laid out New York's Central Park in 1857, also designed the wealthy Philadelphia suburb of Chestnut Hill and in doing so enshrined what has been called the greatest of American suburban landscape institutions, the front lawn. At Chestnut Hill, the boulevards were lined with trees; high walls or fences were forbidden; and each house was set back at least ten metres from the front lot line. The result was a visually unbroken greensward that embraced and unified every lot in the block. The collective savanna appealed enormously to American notions of wide-open spaces and democratic equality. Thus the American lawn embraced the Wild West, aristocratic pretensions, and a noisy new egalitarianism.

In 1870 the definitive catechism of lawnery appeared in the form of Frank J. Scott's landmark work, *The Art of Beautifying Suburban Home Grounds*. Scott minced no words: "A smooth, closely-shaven surface of grass is by far the most essential element of beauty on the grounds of a suburban house." Nor should lawns be cluttered up with fussy flower beds or garish displays: Scott urged the new suburbanites to "let your lawn be your home's velvet robe, and your flowers not too promiscuous decorations."

With these admonitions ringing in their ears, North America's middle classes set out to transform forest and field, highland and hollow into one great unbroken lawn of the imagination. On the unlikely grounds of the suburban lawnscape, crazy, guilt-wracked, ambivalent America reached its compromise with wilderness. But, despite Scott's sober admonishments, "promiscuous decorations" started popping up everywhere. Rotting rowboats planted in petunias, wagon wheels, and other *objets trouvées* rescued from the vanishing rural landscape found new life as lawn ornaments. Folk-art statuary became a growth industry, populating the continent with hideous replications of timid deer, cavorting gnomes, and corpulent toads. I once lived in an upscale suburb of New York City where lawn after lawn featured an outdoor lamp held aloft by a grinning little black man dressed as a jockey. Fountains and sundials and sham-marble birdbaths abound. Religious icons, fake wishing wells, even plastic tree stumps—there's an ornament for every taste. North Americans spend an estimated 4 billion bucks a year just on lawn ornaments. Here on our little island, one of the neighbours created either an all-time low in tastelessness or a brilliant satirical comment on these ornamental excesses by unabashedly mounting on twin entrance posts, like lions rampant, two old white toilet bowls planted with red pelargoniums. Bravo!

But how much do lawns really contribute to the pursuit of happiness? The reviews are mixed at best. Home-owners probably spend more time complaining about lawns than about any other part of their properties. Small wonder. Trying to duplicate the greenswards of dripping Britain in Scottsdale, Arizona, or Coboconk, Ontario, means bracing oneself for a Promethean struggle against local growing conditions. "Grassation" is an obsolete English term meaning "the making of violent assaults," and getting grass to grow where it naturally will not involves repeated assaults against the local growing regime. Chemical fertilizers, moss killers, lime, broadleaf herbicides, relentless irrigation: all get poured on, year after year. Nature, in turn, assaults the misplaced lawn with droughts, frosts, floods, chewing insects, genetically improved weeds, dog droppings, pedestrian shortcuts, and similar indignities. "Keep Off the Grass" becomes the primal scream of the lawn owner too often battered by pitiless fate. The lucky ones learn to laugh in the face of disaster: grass, says the old joke, is the green stuff that wilts on the lawn and thrives in the garden.

Never mind. The tending of lawns is not a matter of personal choice. It has evolved into something else entirely, both a collective compulsion and an obligation of good citizenship. To shirk that community obligation is to court disaster. Consider the case of poor Fred and Venda Bytendorp of Salt Lake City, Utah. In 1992 the Bytendorps killed their lawn by spraying it with a defoliant, and then boasted to a city inspector that the action was a protest against high water rates. Not amused, officials promptly charged the rebels with "failure to maintain their landscape," an offence punishable by thirty days in jail and a thousand-dollar fine.

Even when officialdom fails to notice criminal behaviour on the premises, the neighbours will. Peer pressure for proper maintenance of lawns is a force mightier than the atom. Sandy's father, Bill, unleashed it once. A respected member of a respectable neighbourhood in Victoria on Vancouver Island, Bill simply stopped mowing his back lawn, in plain view of a half-dozen neighbouring homes. The grass shot up like a hayfield. Co-conspirators, we donated a bucket of garter snakes to occupy this wonderful new "wild garden." But soon the grumbling started, and the great wheel of community disapproval began to grind slowly in Bill's direction. Seized by an uncharacteristic spirit of devil-may-care, Bill dragged out his mower and mowed a large heart-shaped area in the centre of the lawn as a tribute to his wife upon her return from hospital. The rest he left as wild as before. You could almost hear indignation crackling through the neighbourhood. Disapproval hung in the air like smoke.

An easy-going and accommodating fellow, Bill began to bend before this awesome force. Eventually, his wildness spent, he caved in and restored the lawn to its former well-kept decency. If one grows grass, the message is unmistakable, one keeps it trimmed. A badly maintained lawn is admissible evidence of sloth and failure, of moral rot infesting the ownership. Worse, it signals the thin edge of a weedy wedge which, unless repulsed, will drive the entire neighbourhood inevitably into the greedy clutches of slumlords.

Despite the massive forces of deterrence arrayed against them, there are still those who would defy convention, who chafe against the ritual of lawn mowing, sprinkling, fertilizing, liming, weeding, and edging. Besides the ill-considered forms of rebellion attempted by Bill and the Bytendorps (entirely cowed, the latter pleaded that they'd killed their lawn "by mistake" and that any talk of protest was "only a joke"), other anti-lawn gambits have proven at least marginally successful. These are generally divided into two categories: suburban subrealism, which coats the entire yard with concrete, coloured pebbles, bark mulch, or some other inert substance in which no living thing survives; and, at the opposite pole, rustic idealism, which encourages a "natural" lawn, precursor to the full-blown "wild" garden. Sham ruralism is much in vogue at present, and is considered more environmentally sound than coloured pebbles.

A natural lawn, as opposed to a lawn "let go," is planted with particular grass species that are supposed to grow slowly through the spring, reach their apex by midsummer, and fade away by fall. A romantic variation is the wildflower meadow in which seeds of assorted wildflowers are cast about and left to fight it out with the clover and crabgrass. In its highest form, the wildflower meadow features a barefoot young woman who looks like Elvira Madigan running perpetually through it. Experts recommend that a natural lawn be cut only twice a year, like a hayfield. But how to cut it? Scything is an option with honourable roots, and the 'burbs might be wonderfully enlivened by the sight of muscular citizens smoothly scything their lawns. But Eleanor Perényi prudently warns that "scything is an exercise that might easily kill the average suburban home-owner who already has trouble with the power mower."

A second difficulty with natural lawns stems from the inability of certain neighbours to distinguish between a badly maintained regular lawn and an impeccably maintained natural one. Despite extraordinary diligence, a natural lawn can appear to suspicious minds to be an outgrowth of negligence. Even a wildflower meadow, after its three weeks of bloom, can look treacherously like the product of old-fashioned indolence hiding behind the shrubbery of political correctness.

It might be thought that the ultimate solution lies in getting out of view of any neighbours and feeling free to do whatever you want. Don't believe it. At our place, we're completely surrounded by woods; the little clearing which contains our house, gardens, orchard, and outbuildings is something less than a hectare all told, and has perhaps half a hectare of lawns around all the various components. About an acre by my rough reckoning. But I beg you to believe that this grassy expanse is no pseudo-aristocratic conceit. It's a matter of survival. A temporary beachhead against the jungle out there. Let a couple of seasons go by in which no grass is cut, and rank growth will seize the open ground with unbelievable ferocity. Huge Himalayan blackberry bushes lurk on the perimeter like murderous thugs, waiting to break and enter. Armed and dangerous salmonberry canes shake their thorny sticks at us and threaten insurrection.

Encircled by menacing hordes, new pilgrims in a savage land, we defend our little outpost by periodic mowing. Once upon a time we cherished the illusion of maintaining this grassy Maginot Line as a classical greensward, the sort of place where Capability Brown could wander about comfortably. To begin with, we bought an el-cheapo rotary power mower to realize the vision. Underpowered and altogether pathetic, the little machine coughed and spluttered and stalled so often the job became almost full-time. We traded up to a second-hand 3.5-h.p. rear-bagger that ripped and tore its way through the grass and repeatedly clogged up with grassy pulp. About every two minutes, I'd have to stop the machine, remove and empty the bag, tip the mower and remove the pulp clogging the blades, replace the bag, and try restarting the motor. Sensing a weakness, rank weeds began infesting the lawn; the perimeter line showed signs of tottering; the surrounding jungle chuckled.

Two things saved us from what could have been a very ugly end: appropriate technology and readjustment of attitude. We acquired a second-hand reel mower with fifty-centimetre blades, five horsepower, and a drive wheel that could power through the defensive line of the Buffalo Bills. It's the kind of machine many professional lawn maintenance people use; it's fast, unstoppable, and tremendously fuel-efficient. The scissoring action of a reel mower cuts the tips of grass far more cleanly than the sloppy bludgeoning of a rotary mower. And, best of all, the blades flip the clippings into a metal hopper in front which can be quickly emptied while the mower idles, purrs almost, like a Mercedes Benz. The fresh-cut clippings make an invaluable mulch for vegetable and flower beds—thereby radically reducing weeding and watering requirements—and a useful activator for compost heaps. As well, we tell ourselves, vigorous running behind the machine is excellent for the cardiovascular system. One needs at least three or four sound arguments in defence of this massive mowing in order to deflect the cruel jibes of zealots who question its environmental appropriateness.

But of course the critics have a point, and it's here where a change of attitude helps enormously. We're conditioned to think that grass and only grass should be permitted in a lawn, that mosses and dandelions and daisies are clear evidence that we too are falling behind, succumbing to slovenliness, going to the dogs. But, short of using herbicides, there's no realistic way of preventing other plants from sharing the lawn space. Moist corners are populated by various feather mosses whose spores drift in from the forest. In sunnier spots, white clover and dandelions cohabit with the grasses. For years I saw these invaders as creeping blights, agents of imperfection. But then the deer taught me otherwise.

Several small families of blacktail deer browse on our lawns. Every day from early spring until winter they wander around the lawns, cropping the turf. Some days, glancing up from a garden chore, you'd think we were on the Serengeti Plains, there are so many ungulates munching contentedly. Two of their favourite foods, I realized after lengthy observation, are clovers and dandelions. Suddenly, like Saul on the road to Damascus, I was struck by a great insight: these pernicious "weeds" over which we'd been fretting serve some purpose after all. From there it was a small imaginative leap to recognizing that white clover—although it is a nuisance in flower beds and rockwork—is a fine nitrogen fixer and is actually enriching the lawn soil, which is more than we do. The tap roots of dandelions and similar plants enrich soil too, bringing nutrients up from the subsoil. As if by magic, the lawn that had for so long bedevilled us with self-recrimination because it was so weedy became instead a source of delight. The flowers of clover, dandelion, and daisy were transformed from vexatious weeds to components of a quite acceptable and environmentally sound ground cover.

We mow the lawns perhaps six times a year now, mostly in the exuberant growth spurts of spring. Except for two tiny patches inside the flower garden, we don't aerate, lime, fertilize, dethatch or weed at all, and never water any of it. For the most part, we just let it be, more a meadow than a lawn, where deer browse contentedly and where frogs and snakes find cover in the longish grasses. When things get too unkempt-looking, I wheel out the big reel mower, set as high as possible, and trim it all back down again.

The disconcerting part is this: no matter how thoroughly one appreciates intellectually the wisdom of breaking from North America's lawn fetish, of rejecting the obsession with "a smooth, closely-shaven surface of grass" and all the high-nitrogen fertilizers, herbicides, and water wastage that goes into its maintenance, still, when the mowing's done and the mounds of precious clippings are barrowed to the garden, leaving a fresh, trim carpet of grass, I feel a bizarre little thrill of satisfaction, of emotional well-being. I don't know if it's some genetic hankering for the ancestral savannas of Africa, or simple nostalgia for the sweeping parkland greenswards of my English childhood, or the serenity of personal redemption for creating orderliness and harmony in a wild, inchoate world. Or none of the above. I realize that the feeling, although undeniable, is foolish. And temporary. The blackberry vines and the bracken, I know, and eventually the forest primeval, will triumph in the end.

10

Money

"*But*, darling!" exclaimed the shocked lady upon being told by her son that he intended to make gardening his profession, "a gardener is something one has, not something one is." This anecdote was told by an acquaintance who, after making a great success of restoring formal gardens in England, could well afford to chuckle at his mother's misgivings over his choice of profession. Frankly, I suspect him of having purloined the punchline from someone like Somerset Maugham.

The Monty Python gang used to sing, "there is nothing quite as wonderful as money," but few things are more problematic for the gardener. Poor soil we can amend, foul weather deflect by our cleverness, headstrong plants head back. But money means mischief whichever side of the coin comes up. Too much of it can overwhelm a garden as surely as too little may impoverish it. And the perils of practical cash flow are just the beginning. A garden's ledger also includes all sorts of arcane entries concerning wealth, power, and class. Anyone who has put foot to fork realizes that throughout history the gardens we now think of as great were the conceptions of wealthy people executed by hordes of far less wealthy workers. Alhambra, the renaissance papal garden in Rome, Hampton Court—each served as both instrument and symbol of class privilege. Today, with millions of people confined in highrise apartments, and thousands sleeping in refrigerator cartons under bridges, those of us with even a little patch of dirt to putter in find ourselves numbered among a privileged elite.

For guilt-wracked Catholics like myself, for socialists, retrofitted communists, and humanitarians generally, this is not good. We ask ourselves: Did I hang a Che Guevara poster on my revolutionary walls all those years, only to end up a complacent member of the landowning classes, fiddling with primulas while the world burns? With the price of the tackiest townhouses spiralling out of reach for more and more people, the guilt-ridden gardener begins feeling like some obese Guatemalan land baron living on the backs of starving *campesinos*. You take to staring in the bathroom mirror, looking for any resemblance to those French aristocrats of the seventeenth century who would routinely have whole villages demolished in order to extend the uncluttered vistas of their estate gardens.

Liberal misgivings about privilege do at least serve one useful purpose: they curb that destroyer of ambitious gardens, wealthy ostentation. Properties whose principal function is to advertise the importance of their owners may succeed as advertisements, but they're invariably miserable gardens. The classic of the genre is Versailles, and I like Henry Mitchell's verdict on that unfortunate expanse of exhibitionism: "I remember at Versailles, the garden of Louis XIV, wondering how anybody could spend so much money and construct canals on so large a scale and have so many trees and still achieve a sparse and stingy look."

As the Sun King undoubtedly knew, one of the privileges of those who can afford chequebook gardening is that they can appropriate other people's labour as though it were their own. So you'll have someone announce, rather grandly, over cocktails, "I planted a little copse of weeping purple beeches in the lawn last week." Well, not really. What the speaker actually did was direct hired labourers to dig the holes, prepare the planting mix, plant and stake the trees, and clean up the mess on the lawn afterwards. This is a handy way of establishing ownership of work without actually working up a sweat. And it allows for a genteel reinforcement of the comforting notion that the unequal distribution of wealth in the world is a dispensation of Providence that one is compelled, however reluctantly, to accept. In some households, perhaps suffering reduced circumstances, disgruntled husbands are substituted for hired hands to much the same effect.

The love of riches, as Cicero told us long ago, is characteristic of a narrowness and littleness of soul. The insolence of wealth leaches charm out of a garden as surely as incessant rain leaches out nutrients. Knowing this full well still doesn't prevent us penny-ante plantspeople from aping the landscapes of the great estates of yesteryear. We'll dream of creating a fabulous garden in the style of a Georgian country house, and spend long hours poring over the writings of Gertrude Jeckyll. What does it matter that virtually all the Jeckyll-inspired gardens long ago expired from want of the enormous amounts of money and skilled labour required to sustain them? We'll plunge in just the same, confident that with our after-tax earnings and a high-school kid working for minimum wage we can duplicate the gardens that once crowned an empire.

We are advised, wisely, by garden writers to shun any show of wealth in the garden, to exclude anything that is more expensive or elaborate than necessary. This is the kind of financial planning I like. With no wealth to show, not showing it becomes a reasonably easy thing. I was raised in a family in which penny-pinching was elevated to a fine art, so that parsimony comes almost as second nature. Over the years, Sandy—who grew up with a relatively healthy attitude towards money—has been gradually seduced by the cheap attractions of thrift. Cost effectiveness is the catchword at our place, a fiscal prudence in comparison to which Thatcherism looks like philanthropy. Not long ago we might have been ostracized as skinflints, niggards, miserable pinchfists. But mercifully, the environmental movement has cast a new and nobler light upon miserliness. Nowadays we're all encouraged to "do better with less," to "reduce, reuse, and recycle." After years of scuttling furtively down back alleys from the Goodwill store to the Sally Ann in search of second-hand bargains, suddenly it's chic to be thrifty. There are BMWs in the thrift-shop lot. At long last pinchpennies can come out of the closet!

Chic or not, thriftiness has its price in the garden. Take the matter of implements. The parsimonious gardener is constantly on the lookout for a bargain in tools. Not long ago I emerged triumphantly from our local Goodwill store, the proud new owner of an ancient pole pruner. With a long hardwood handle and pre-industrial wire apparatus for engaging the cutting blade inside a beak-like hook, this contraption appears to have been hand-fashioned by some desperate homesteader in the bleakest years of the nineteenth century. But for us it represented a state-of-the-art technological breakthrough. Previously, high-wire pruning had involved either scrambling around in the branches of the target tree with secateurs and saw in hand, or balancing suicidally on the topmost rung of a geriatric stepladder. Nowadays I can stand gracefully on the ground, raise my antique pruner like the lance of a knight errant entering the joust, and by forcefully yanking on its primitive handle snip off sky-bound water shoots with ease. It's true that you can buy contemporary models of the same device fashioned from aluminum, incredibly light and smooth-operating, with a ratcheted blade that could sever a giant sequoia—but you can't get it for five bucks.

Whatever small economies can be realized in pruning come as a godsend, because generally pruning represents a startling deficit on the gardening spreadsheet. Here I'm talking about the secateur cycle, a grim law of garden economics which decrees that no pair of hand pruners shall remain in one's possession long enough to justify their purchase price. Secateurs are like kids' mittens: unless you secure them to something, they'll slip away the instant your back's turned. We've gone through dozens of them, and many a lively discussion has erupted over who was the numbskull who last used, and lost, the latest pair. Who knows where old secateurs go? Every so often a rusty old pair will show up in the compost heap, but mostly they seem to just vanish into thin air, like hapless craft entering the Bermuda Triangle.

With this radically shortened shelf life, secateurs must be purchased often and with extreme care. You hardly want to go forking over the family inheritance for a titanium-plated model with mother-of-pearl handgrips, only to lose them within nanoseconds of their first engagement. Far wiser to stick with cut-rate imitations from Taiwan which are designed to never produce a clean cut, but which regularly and painfully scrunch your fingernails. Losing a pair of these brutes can become a genuine cause for celebration. In the matter of secateurs, the smart money long ago learned to cut its losses, buy cheap, and keep moving.

Would that things were as simple in the tangled world of water pipes! Our far-flung plantings demand a dozen different hose outlets, and we own one ancient but admirable rubber hose along with eight or nine cheap plastic ones. The couplings on these are invariably worn and impossible to tighten, so that when you turn the water on, a nasty spray gushes from the connection and gives you a cold soaking. The hoses themselves are usually pliable enough if they've been lying in the hot sun all day, but the run of cold water soon cools them down, rendering them stiff and inflexible. Then the kinks kick in. You'll be watering away happily, your imagination dancing lightly among the radishes and rutabagas, when the water flow abruptly stops. Six metres back the hose has kinked, blocking the water flow. You flick the hose, bullwhip style, neatly severing the heads from several nearby plants, but failing to undo the kink. You put the hose down, walk back to the kink and straighten it out, resulting in a sudden gush of water blasting out of the nozzle right at your most prized seedlings, the way cops aim fire hoses at rioters. Sometimes the hose will thrash around like a worm that's just been cut in half, knocking plants about in its writhings. Soaked anew, you seize the hose and resume watering, though less happily. As soon as you move a few steps the hose kinks again.

After a few seasons of this nonsense, any gardener would lose patience. You deserve better, and you head straight to the hardware store determined to buy better. You spot what you want: a good reinforced rubber hose.

Then you see the price tag and pause for a moment. Doubt assails you. A dozen of these beauties could push the budget deficit to an insupportable depth. You vacillate. You inch along to where the "budget-priced" hoses are displayed. Costing a third as much as the luxury models, they're within your budgetary guidelines. But you ask yourself: why spend good money on something that's no better than what we already have? Frugality rules. You convince yourself that you'll eventually find the perfect hose at a garage sale or store liquidation sale somewhere. I've been telling myself this for twenty years. And, astoundingly, believing it.

For the parsimonious gardener, hoses aren't the only thing that's kinky. There's the much larger field of acquiring plants for minimum cash outlay, and here the horizon is all but limitless. The operative principle is to never spend dollars on a plant when the same thing can be had by spending cents on a seed, and never buy seed if a cutting or rooting can be had for free. In his prime, my little Irish father was a marvel at helping himself to seed heads and softwood cuttings wherever he wandered. Having years ago worked as a professional gardener in English parks, he loved to roam through public parks and gardens, and if a particular plant took his fancy, he'd whip out his penknife and cut himself a few slips, which he'd wrap in damp kleenex. Ripe seed heads were also fair game. As a son and non-gardener, I was mortified. Nowadays, as my own passion for plants has far outstripped my cash flow, I've come to better appreciate the merits of the seed head, free for the plucking, and of the Irish cutting.

Even more productively, we took to prowling the countryside in search of gardens about to be demolished because they lay in the path of progress. There's nothing quite so forlorn as a derelict garden awaiting the bulldozer's blade. Many's the time we've excavated trees, shrubs, and perennials, literally snatching them from the cruel jaws of earth-moving equipment and carrying them home to a renewed chance at life. Here again the highest principles of frugality and environmentalism happily coincide.

However, when shopping at nurseries, the prescriptions of thrift are often in peril. We're all familiar with the seductive charms of nursery stock, and normally the parsimonious gardener enjoys a distinct advantage over spendthrifts, because few things guarantee garishness in the garden more surely than impulse buying in a nursery. The compulsion to load up on whatever catches one's fancy at the moment can be positively toxic to garden homogeneity. Tightfistedness resists these fatal attractions. But nowadays plant prices can fluctuate as wildly as pork belly futures, and comparison shopping is an absolute must. Increasingly, nurseries are behaving like supermarkets, with sales events at which advertised plants are discounted as loss leaders.

The fiscal line of defence against eclectic impulses may falter entirely when there's an out-and-out giveaway going on. Not long ago a large nursery near us began a total renovation, and chose to liquidate its entire growing stock to facilitate the changeover. Everything was discounted 70 per cent. Recession-battered plantspeople poured in from all over the district. We all had a slightly feverish gleam in our eyes, and we wheeled our overloaded carts around with the frenzied giddiness of those people who've won five minutes free shopping at a supermarket. Sandy and I staggered out with larger trees than we'd ever bought before. Our van was jammed with bargains, and it wasn't until the sober light of the following day that we realized our enthusiasm had embraced a number of plants questionably suited to our purposes.

But who can resist a bargain? If there's no sale on, we'll skulk around the perimeters of nurseries seeking out half-dead or derelict plants that can be had for a song. Sometimes this works wonderfully. On one occasion, for mere pennies, we bought a pussy willow bearing striking black catkins with red anthers *(Salix gracilistyla melanostachys)*. It was an undeniably decrepit-looking specimen, and the salespeople arched their eyebrows over our Mexican marketplace haggling about how little we should pay to take it off their hands. But we knew that few things have a lust for life that can equal a young willow's, and we made our escape brimming with confidence. Sure enough, released from its root-binding pot and planted in a boggy spot near the creek, the willow took off like a rocket.

Not every find is quite so rewarding. At another nursery we were advancing the cause of recycling and reusing by liberating a bundle of discarded plastic flats from a dumpster when we spotted a real treasure: a large potted San Jose juniper which had been carefully clipped and pruned into an elegant shape. Alive it would be worth at least fifty or sixty dollars. But was it alive? I fished it out of the dumpster and detected sufficient signs of life to justify an attempt at resuscitation. We planted it in an intensive care unit, watered it, pampered it, talked to it, caressed it lovingly, did everything but give it a coronary bypass. But in vain! Its life-force was already spent, and the best we could do for it was cast it on a funeral pyre, which at least saved it from the indignity of the dumpster.

Disease and poverty, as we know, cohabit the same squalid quarters, and the gravest risk of horticultural dumpster diving is that you might introduce some dreadful disease into your garden. As a cautionary tale, I offer you our calamity with kalmias. Early in spring we picked up a pair of sale-priced kalmias at a nursery. They looked all right at the time, but after a few weeks in our rhododendron garden they sickened and blackened as though they had the vegetative equivalent of leprosy. I yanked them out rudely and consigned them to the purifying fire. But too late! Our previously healthy rhodos soon began to suffer from the same creeping black plague of a disease. We can't quite determine whether it's anthracnose or some genetically improved blight, but it's got its filthy fingers into all the broad-leafed evergreens and threatens to stay with us until it has finally blackened them all.

In such cases, of course, you can return plants to the

nursery where you bought them and request a replacement. This, however, should be done with extreme care in order to avoid public embarrassment. In certain instances a wig and sunglasses are advisable. Not long ago we marched purposively into a nursery with a potted camellia and a viburnum, neither of which appeared to have survived their first winter with us. The nursery manager looked us over appraisingly, whipped out a knife and scraped a small patch from the stem of each plant. A telltale bit of green showed. "There!" she announced triumphantly, "they're both still alive." Her tone implied that we'd had embezzlement on our minds. A disapproving murmur ran through the line of sullen customers behind us, as though we'd been caught at insider trading. We reclaimed our near-dead plants and slunk away in disgrace.

Not long ago I saw a newspaper report outlining how a professor at the University of Calcutta had calculated the financial leverage of a common tree. Living for fifty years, according to the professor, a tree produces $31,250 worth of oxygen; recycles $37,500 worth of water; creates $31,250 worth of soil fertility; provides $62,000 worth of air pollution abatement and $31,250 worth of shelter for animals. Not counting fruit, shade or aesthetic values, a common tree is worth about $200,000 by this peculiar reckoning.

We have to applaud the professor's objective—developing an economic argument to justify not cutting down every tree on the horizon. But I fear it's a rationale with a built-in backlash. If money becomes the ground of argument, and another investment strategist can demonstrate that a billboard standing there instead of a tree will generate twice as much revenue over the same period, it won't be long before the chain saw sings. This, in capsule form, is the history of post-conquest North America.

I've come to the conclusion that gardeners are far better off remaining entirely aloof from the financial obsession of our times. We should decline to measure everything against "the bottom line," because a garden seldom submits happily to cost-benefit analysis. Take beans, for example, as Thoreau did in his short-lived stint at Walden Pond. Most everyone agrees that beans are beautiful—easy to plant, happy in the roughest ground, magnificent in their emergence from the earth, undemanding of water or fertilizer, generous in fixing nitrogen in the soil, easy to harvest, shell, and store, their spent plants excellent in compost heaps.

Big on beans of all kinds, Sandy and I grow several varieties of green and wax beans each year. My favourite is an elegantly slender French snap bean called 'Aramis'. Bean salads are a mainstay on hot summer days, and we freeze big bags of green and yellow snap beans for winter soups. Broad beans are a staple: we dry and freeze lots of them, and process others into a bean paste for use as a spread or in homemade homous.

From these successes, even by an accountant's reckoning, I grew inordinately enthusiastic about beans and determined to meet the full spectrum of our bean needs. Soya beans, kidney beans, black beans, shell beans—we tried them all. Realistically, our summers are a tad too cool for many of these sun lovers, and none have overwhelmed us with their abundance. A bit offended by their lacklustre performance, last year I made the mistake of looking at a bed of 'Walcherse' white shell beans from the unforgiving perspective of the bottom line. Any auditor would have been aghast. Consider: time is expended in perusing catalogues and ordering seed stock, digging over and raking their bed, planting, and watering until they were well underway. We weeded the bed twice, and followed the second weeding with a heavy mulch of grass clippings. A few more waterings were needed through the season. In late summer we cropped them off, composted the plants, and dug the bed over again. Lastly we spent an hour or two shelling the small pods. The end result of perhaps ten hours of work? About two dollars' worth of dried beans.

Yes, I know, this is the moment to trot out every convenient rationale: that these beans are certifiably organic; that we're helping save the planet by living a non-consumer lifestyle through "growing our own"; that we stand in solidarity with the rural poor worldwide who survive largely on beans, rice, and corn; that I benefitted from the wholesome exercise of digging, and thoroughly enjoyed the whole process.

Still, it's hard to avoid the nagging reality that you've been working for twenty cents an hour. For a luscious ripe organic tomato that bursts lasciviously all over your lips you wouldn't cavil. Or for the fleeting sweetness of fresh-picked corn, no question. But for a bag of dried beans? Bean people will object, zealots that they are, but there seemed to me something unavoidably demeaning about it. I wasn't sure that I hadn't been exploited in some way. Unfortunately, in these circumstances, you're both management and labour, and you can hardly accuse yourself of being a meanspirited bean-counter.

This, in turn, raises the whole question of hired help in the garden. I myself have had considerable experience as a hired hand, but none whatsoever as a person doing the hiring. Judging by the grumbling, good help is impossible to find nowadays. As Eleanor Perényi laments: "When I look on the long procession of incompetents, dumbbells and eccentrics, young and old, foreign and domestic, who have worked for me, I wonder how I and the garden have survived their ministrations." The dream, of course, is that you'll discover some fantastically knowledgeable person from the old country, or some grand master of Zen gardening anxious to do your bidding in exchange for a bowl of soup and a few kind words. Instead you're apt to get a hulking oaf who is scarcely capable of cutting grass but whose hourly rate would be the envy of most corporate lawyers.

Not long ago I observed a hired hand at work in a friend's yard in the city. This character has horticultural credentials up one arm and down the other, and is considered a steal at twenty dollars an hour. His technique was magnificent, and devoted largely to contemplation of the task at hand. Called upon to shear a cedar hedge, he wielded his instruments with the dexterity of a brain surgeon. He snipped once, stood back, considered, went to snip again, paused, reconsidered, eventually snipped again. The twenty-minute chore was elaborated into a profound meditation upon the essence of cedarness and hedgeness that was still in progress when I departed several hours later.

Which brings us full circle to the maternal advice that a gardener is something one has, not something one is. When asked in social circumstances, "and what do you do?", it's simply not acceptable to reply, "I garden." Believe me, I've tried it. An awkward silence ensues, smiles wobble, people bolt to the bathroom or bar. You'd be better received if you said you specialize in hostile corporate takeovers.

This social pressure helps explain the deluge of gardening books on the racks nowadays. To rise from the social opprobrium attached to a career in gardening, up to modest stardom, all a person has to do is write a gardening book. How marvellous to be able to respond to social enquiry with a nonchalant, "Oh, I'm an author." Squeals of delight. Fawning. Outrageous flattery. Naturally, it's best not to volunteer that you've written a gardening book; a cryptic "non-fiction" has far deeper intellectual resonance.

Why gardeners are ostracized while writers are lionized is as plain as pansies: nowadays, gardening, unlike most writing, is a profoundly subversive activity. Corporate investment strategists and financial services conglomerates recognize in gardening the seeds of sedition. Everything that gardening represents—leisure, delight in the moment, contemplative repose, simplicity, humility, silence, love of the natural world—these are anathema to the corporate elites for whom the world turns.

Most gardeners are more excited about seed catalogues than corporate loan portfolios; they don't give two hoots about a credit rating downgrade if the *Magnolia grandiflora* is in bloom.

How can a convertible debenture compete against a drift of alstroemeria? Well, it can't. Imagine the blow to investor confidence if corporate strategists could open their sealed windows and smell the violets?

Living at peace with themselves and the natural world, bona fide gardeners have no need for the ambitious aggression so prized in a predatory economic culture. They simply don't go along with the desolation of nature, the disintegration of the human spirit, that pass for progress. The gardens of the nation are fertile breeding grounds for paradigm shifts, for revolutionary attitudes, and the money managers are right to quake in their Armani jackets at the prospect of flower power eventually unleashed.

11

Weeds

*C*ertain people insist upon making irritating statements about weeds. You'll be down on your hands and knees, fingers scratched and psyche near sapped from long hours spent pulling at pernicious weeds, when one of these types will smile at you benignly from the patio and inform you that a weed is, after all, merely a plant in the wrong place. Grrrrr. Or you'll be flat on the grass, writhing in agony from a herniated disk twisted in a too strenuous tug of war with some monstrously taprooted dock plant, when one of these dilettantes will enquire as to whether you've much pondered Emerson's thought that a weed is simply a plant whose virtues haven't yet been discovered.

Gardeners as a group have not received sufficient

acknowledgement for their restraint towards these provocateurs. Nobody knows the ways of weeds more thoroughly than a gardener does, nobody less requires telling about the virtues and vices of vegetation. The misunderstood species described so mytho-poetically by our philosophical friends are the civilized and dainty weeds, those that introduce themselves discreetly, never becoming vulgar, brash, or pushy. Finding them in inappropriate locations, we pick them out and toss them away as though we were idly gathering meadow daisies for a chain. We might whistle a little Mendelssohn as we pluck them from the rose garden. I think of lamb's-quarters in this way—an altogether discreet and civilized visitor, and undeserving of its nicknames: pigweed, muckweed, dungweed, and fat hen. All Good they called it in the old days, when its beneficial properties made it perhaps the most important vegetable in the human diet. Today we think of it less well, partly because of its weedy penchant for showing up uninvited in places where it's not wanted. But it is easily removed and never vindictive after rejection.

More apt to test the gardener's mettle, couch grass is another of those once-useful plants now fallen from grace and become a nuisance. A globe-trotting troublemaker—known variously as witch grass, twitch grass, quick grass and scrutch grass—it disperses by seed and then colonizes an area with a mat of creeping rhizomes. The pointed tip of a rhizome can easily penetrate right through a potato or a piece of wood. Or pierce your heart, for it spreads through the garden faster than gossip at an office party. We slash at these coarse grasses with machete, scythe, and sickle, rip the rhizomes out with spade, fork, and grub hoe. But still it advances, each year infesting a few new pockets on the garden periphery. We flail away on the open and most easily defended turf, but the grass hops in behind an old stump, lurks in rock piles, under fences and other dark corners we can't contest.

In the heat of battle you don't much care that couch grass's name derives from an old Anglo-Saxon word for "vivacious," and that its subversive rhizomes were once commonly sold in markets as a remedy for all sorts of ills. Dog's grass they used to call this wildling too, because ailing dogs will instinctively nibble its foliage. I've often seen our old border collie, Fen, eat the leaves and then vomit, I think as a way of disgorging hair balls. Seventeenth-century herbalist Nicholas Culpeper wrote: "If you do not know it by this description, watch the dogs when they are sick, and they will quickly lead you to it." Around our place there's no need to go to the dogs to find it, for each year this witch's grass advances a little more brashly, a little more brazenly towards the heart of our gardens.

And then there are the real thugs among weeds, the ones with no apparent redeeming social value. These ruffians roam about in gangs, barging in where they're not wanted, unruly gatecrashers at the garden party. Voices are raised. Pushing and shoving ensues. Curses stain the air. Fresh earth is kicked up. Some hothead threatens somebody with a hoe, and before cooler heads can prevail, gang warfare breaks out.

Several groups of these hooligans menace our neighbourhood. Perhaps the most vicious is the trailing blackberry, a long and thorny tripwire that can stretch seven
metres or more. Armed to the teeth and tough as a pit
bull, trailing blackberry invades our place with the
impunity of a tribal warlord. Its sinewy tentacles reach
forward in a single season, root themselves, reach forward again and again root. You wanna fight about it? they
seem to sneer. Yank on one of the invasive arms and it
simply snaps off, leaving the root behind, stimulated to
multiply, and leaving you frustrated—and tortured for
your trouble by a handful of tiny thorns. The glove has
yet to be manufactured through which these infernal
little thorns can't penetrate. This is a weed with attitude.
Its hatefulness threatens to erode one's firm resolve to
not use herbicides. Embattled and impaled, you hear the
devil whisper in your ear that you need merely dip the tip
of this heinous vine in a bottle of 2,4-D and that systemic
killer will blight the whole thing like the wrath of
Jehovah. Trapped in this murderous moral quandary, the
last thing you need to hear is some Saturday-afternoon
pansy planter mouthing quotations from James Russell
Lowell that a weed is simply "a flower in disguise."

But what is a weed really? My *Oxford Dictionary* defines
it as "a herbaceous plant not valued for use or beauty,
growing wild and rank, and regarded as cumbering the
ground or hindering the growth of superior vegetation."
The definition drips with subjective judgements: "val-

ued," "regarded," and "superior." Are weeds merely plants about which we humans have opinions? Are those infuriating acquaintances so fond of quoting Emerson and Lowell actually correct? Rank growth we can all agree with, but that could equally be said of alstroemeria, rambling roses, English ivy, or any number of other plants. No, the real problem is that a weed does not look attractive to us. It usurps ground that we believe could support more useful or appealing plants. British horticulturalist Beth Chatto advises that "all gardeners have to make up their own minds about what they consider to be a weed in their garden and whether they can tolerate it." What decides the issue in Chatto's opinion, "is whether the plant in question harms the rest of the planting."

Gardeners don't do well with this type of moral relativism, for it flings us willy-nilly into a briar patch of thorny questions about human interference with natural processes and can threaten the metaphysical underpinnings of gardening itself. If little Johnny-jump-ups keep jumping up where they're not wanted, are they weeds? If Gaia, in her deep wisdom, clothes herself in a cloak of knapweed, who am I to tear it off and leave her naked?

Still the question lingers: what's a weed? The query is never more germane than when a non-gardener has been dragooned into helping you with weeding and succeeds in plucking out every one of your precious seedlings while leaving in place what to you are plainly weeds. And there's a clue: I think most gardeners would agree that persistence, not to say indestructibility, is at the root of weediness. "A plant with nine lives," one old saying calls the weed; "a thriving garden plant," jests another. While your precious lilies languish or your wonderful Wonga-wonga vine wilts, quackgrass and plantain carry on merrily, as though life were a reckless escapade to be lived to the hilt. Some weeds will tolerate a staggering range of conditions, and every gardener has a tale or two to tell of weeds surviving in unbelievable circumstances. In this vein I offer you our concrete-cracking Scotch thistle. While building our present home, we lived in a smaller place on the property, designed to eventually serve as a dairy barn. This temporary shelter had a poured concrete floor and perimeter footings. An infinitesimally small crackline ran between floor and footings, scarcely wide enough for a razor blade to slip in. One day as we sat down for supper, we spied a thistle poking up through the hairline crack. Its seed must have germinated in the packed rubble under the concrete slab, and now here it was, pushing its way up with the weedling's astounding lust for life. Astonished at this thistly persistence, we let the uninvited guest grow. The plant eventually reached a metre high, though it was a sickly anaemic white for want of sunlight. When it finally produced a rather desperate-looking head of flowers, we cut the thing down, but not without profound new respect for the thistle's tenacity.

In our early sodbusting days thistles were a serious menace. Into gardens newly scratched from former bushland, hordes of thistles swept down like bloodlusty piranhas. They sprouted everywhere, their fleshy white roots diving deep into the subsoil. Dig out a single thistle, and the remaining bit of root, the tiniest fragment of root, would throw up half a dozen dauntingly vigorous replacements. We dared not rototill the vegetable patch for fear of slicing up innumerable roots and triggering a population explosion. Plants dug up by hand had to be incinerated; if you left an uprooted thistle lying on the ground, even in direct sunlight, it might remain there for several weeks, shamming death, and then with the first trickle of moisture, sprout afresh and send new roots back into the earth. Thistles make death and resurrection seem as common as chrysanthemums.

Faint hearts might have quailed at the prospect of a life spent fighting what Shakespeare called "hateful docks, rough thistles." But a marvellous thing happened: after three or four years, the thistles gradually faded away. An old-timer had told me to forget about trying to dig them out, to just keep the tops cut off and they'd eventually give up. And they did. Like other pioneer species, thistles love freshly disturbed earth, where mineral soil and topsoil are commingled. At our place, once things settled down to well-mulched pathways and planting beds, the thistles moved on in search of new rough-and-tumble situations, like some footloose western gunslinger always on the move. Watching them leave, I felt like a grizzled sodbuster leaning pensively upon a hoe, a little wiser now about the strange ways of weeds and drifters, nature's reclamation crew, and their roles in plant succession.

A couple of years ago we were puttering around a nearby town in wintertime and beheld a lovely sight: alongside an urban highway stood a grove of deciduous trees, their leafless limbs adorned with large rusty catkins vivid against the sombre winter sky. Of course we had to investigate. We discovered that the trees were growing in the backyard of an abandoned house, one of a row of bungalows condemned to demolition for the sake of a wider highway. A number of sapling offspring were growing in the grove. We scurried back to the house where we were staying, borrowed a spade and returned to the trees on death row. By now we'd determined that they were probably balsam poplars, and that life would be a hollow affair if we didn't have some growing nearby. We dug up half a dozen saplings, bound their rootballs in burlap sacking and shoved them into the back of the van. At home we planted them temporarily in a spare bed in the vegetable garden, a holding action to determine if they would survive the rough handling they'd suffered.

In early spring the new trees broke bud beautifully and we knew that the operation was a success. But wait! What's this strange plant in the bed? At first it looked to be a juvenile delinquent clematis roaming far from home. Or was it a morning glory that had slipped in with the new trees? As we pondered the strange newcomer's identity, it seemed to slither up like a serpent, girdle the sapling's trunk, and reach out to entwine us too. Startled, we looked more closely and saw this aggressor was not alone: there were at least a dozen others twining up the balsam poplars. Suddenly the whole bed seemed a nest of viny vipers. And with a shock of horror we recognized what they were: the dreaded black bindweed!

We already had a bantamweight annual bindweed at our place—a thin-stemmed little pest that twists up pea vines and raspberry canes and casts its seeds everywhere about two or three hours before you go to weed it out. But that little pipsqueak seemed positively quaint compared with this leviathan bindweed we'd now inadvertently introduced. Its vines twined thick as ropes, sturdy as those Tarzan would swing on between trees. Investigating in the soil, we saw that its roots had already spread like a vile cancer for several metres through the bed and under adjacent pathways. A true megalomaniac among weeds, field bindweed can send out enough underground stolons in a single season to cover twenty-five square metres. Now I recalled seeing these monsters in certain Vancouver neighbourhoods. Running in packs with blood-thirsty Himalayan blackberries, they have taken over whole sections of the city. Pedestrians inch past them warily. Bulldozer operators cower at the prospect of trying to clear an infested lot. Paranoid fantasies now assailed us. We imagined the vegetable patch, the whole property, and eventually the entire island infested with this malignant newcomer; and all due to us, as though we'd offered safe haven to a cadre of neo-Nazi skinheads.

I set about excavating the entire site. No paleontologist ever exposed fossilized bones, no archaeologist ever sifted the small secrets of a midden more painstakingly than I went after those pernicious roots. Forewarned that they can reach more than three metres below the surface, I sieved the soil, digging and redigging the bed until I was satisfied that no fragment remained. The heap of roots I burned on a blazing bonfire, and posted sentries to keep watch for any survivors. The poor poplars were banished to a distant outpost where their splashy winter catkins are seldom seen by human eye. Thus does the gardener dance with near-certain disaster.

The story of gardening in colonized North America is a fantastic chronicle of exotic introductions run amok. Our worst weeds are not native plants but imports we've let loose upon the landscape. Crabgrass, clover, creeping buttercup, and the Himalayan blackberries that infest free ground in our part of the world were all brought here from elsewhere. A century ago some homesick high-lander introduced Scotch broom to Vancouver Island and now the stuff is everywhere, its roots reaching halfway to the southern hemisphere.

Purple loosestrife is another of these sentimental favourites that has turned into a botanical bombshell. Writing in her 1893 classic, *How To Know the Wild Flowers*, American author Mrs. William Starr Dana enthuses: "One who has seen an inland marsh in August aglow with this beautiful plant is almost ready to forgive the Old Country some of the many pests she has shipped to our shores in view of this radiant acquisition." A century later, the radiant acquisition has infested wetlands all over the continent, with disastrous consequences for native plants and the creatures which depend upon them. Purple loosestrife is just now getting a toehold out our way, but we're blessed with a local posse determined to track down this outlaw, and I'm confident that their zeal is every bit a match for the loosestrife's. Imagine my humiliation at being informed by one of the vigilantes that the innocent little loosestrife we'd planted beside our garden pool cross-pollinates with the wetland usurper. Our little specimen didn't look capable of colonizing a roadside ditch, much less establishing a floral empire across vast tracts of wetlands, but only an impossible fool would ignore the warnings of the posse.

The gardener learns early to beware of wildlings that can beguile the gullible with a similitude of charm. Like the practised attractiveness of a singles bar swinger, it may be both illusory and dangerously disarming. We have a wild cranesbill around our region, a native geranium that produces sprays of small pink blossoms in spring and has a lovely ferny foliage that turns vivid red in summer. Hankering in our early days for a show of any sort, we allowed ourselves to be charmed by it. What we didn't realize is that this cranesbill is a crack addict, seeding itself exuberantly into impossible nooks and crannies. We wouldn't want to be completely without it, but we're no longer entirely seduced by its petite springtime display. Beware the wildling that blushes too prettily in the spring; give your heart to no plant until you've studied the set of its seeds.

Creeping weeds are often the worst. Besides the aforementioned couch grass, we also suffer a generous infestation of sheep sorrel, a jaunty little perennial with tasty leaves and a root system that just doesn't quit. The tough but slender roots don't snap when yanked upon, and you can often unearth long garlands of sorrel, with little rosettes of leaves strung along the roots.

Among the wickedest of weeds, creeping buttercup spreads malignantly across a surface but also puts down fleshy roots, almost like taproots. Invading lawns and gardens alike, the plant has a reputation for exhausting the soils in which it grows. Creeping buttercup should never be tackled on a day when one is feeling the least bit vulnerable or fragile. They are best left for days of wrath and fury. I suggest waiting until something has really got your blood boiling—for me, the stupid butcheries of the latest war are excellent—then, in a fine rage, one can storm into the garden and have at the buttercups with a vengeance.

For really deep-rooted troublemakers—I'm thinking here of things like dandelions and the Bard's "hateful docks"— prudence sometimes suggests a policy of mutual coexistence. Both docks and dandelions have an uncanny knack for seeding into pathways and stonework, from which they cannot be coaxed short of demolition and wholesale excavation. If you catch them right away as weedlings, they can be plucked out, but an abiding principle in the war on weeds is that the gardener is always at least one step behind the adversary. A weedling that might readily have been extricated yesterday, but was not, is today dug in deeper than a plantar's wart which no amount of probing will dislodge. This is where a new-found tolerance for weeds can work wonders. An example: in front of our house there's an entranceway fashioned from mortared sandstone pieces. In due course, a wild carrot decided to set up house in a frost-created crack between stone and mortar, sending its fleshy taproot deep into the rubble underneath. As vegetable growers know, our garden-variety carrots, which are descended from this wild species, will throw a temper tantrum, split open, divide into myriad rootlets, and refuse to grow anything but hairy if there's a pebble within a ten-metre radius. But their wild ancestors happily put down roots fatter than Chinese radishes into nothing but stone and rubble.

Early on, I pulled at this weed, stomped on it in passing, sheared its top regularly. But the carrot—also called Queen Anne's lace, from the use of its ferny foliage in fashionable hats and decorations during its namesake's reign—waited patiently until my guard was down and then burgeoned into a grand matriarch, a stout dowager of the species. One day by lucky happenstance I came upon some garden lore that described this roadside weed glowingly. Its curative properties have been exploited since ancient days and provide, according to one old herbalist, "a useful defense against the gravel and stone formed by the lithic acid of a gouty disposition." Often this sort of herbal verbiage can provoke more goutiness of disposition than it cures, but on this occasion it provided just what was needed—a veneer of intellectual decency with which to coat the presence of a whopping big weed right at our front doorstep. I went further, bolstering my case with the unassailable correctness of biodiversity: it turns out that Queen Anne's lace provides food for many of the tiny parasitic wasps that prey upon aphids, whiteflies, and other garden pests. Fully committed to this position, we've now come to love these erstwhile weeds for the ethereal beauty of their lacy foliage and their elegant disks of flowers, like finely fretted ivory, which gradually curl up into concave little bird nests full of seeds. We make a point of keeping several large specimens of these biennials in the garden now, and find their flat white flowers play brilliantly against constellations of flowering purple globe thistles.

Sagacious gardeners can profitably spend long winter evenings poring over musty volumes in search of medicinal, religious, philosophical, or folkloric fragments that can be used to justify the leaving of any weeds that defy elimination. In this spirit, my previous book sang a lengthy paeon of praise to the dandelion. Another subterranean survivor that we have had to come to terms with is the horsetail. Communal plants, they flourish down by our little creek, annually pushing up their bizarre segmented shoots, which one writer described as "moth-eaten asparagus." These spore-bearing growths are followed by equally peculiar branching shoots, resembling pine seedlings cross-dressing as lady ferns.

A major problem weed on the prairies, and much hated for invading pasture land where it can poison young horses, field horsetail cannot be controlled by herbicides. Once upon a time we'd dreamed of transforming the verge of our little brook into a Wordsworthian springtime landscape of velvet grasses splashed with hosts of golden daffodils. But the hairy horsetails declined to surrender their turf. No amount of pulling, scything, mowing, or name-calling succeeded in dislodging them. Like docks and bindweed and other worthy adversaries, horsetails reach deep into the earth for anchorage and sustenance. They're botanical icebergs, with their root systems comprising by far the larger part of total plant bulk.

This plainly was another case of "better learn to love 'em." So we were delighted to discover that horsetails are primeval plants, like mosses and ferns, ancient throwbacks to forests where dinosaurs roamed. Horsetails are the sole survivors of a primitive plant family that once included massive specimens whose Carboniferous era corpses helped create coal deposits in many parts of the planet. Once again, suitably informed, we were able to snatch victory from the jaws of defeat in the war on weeds. If somebody asks why we allow these bizarre-looking growths to spoil the tidiness of creek and poolside, we launch into a dissertation on the need for respect towards ancient plant forms that were flourishing upon the earth long before our ancestors had yet learned to walk on their hind legs. And for the ultimate *coup de grâce*, one can nonchalantly mention that horsetail tea makes a superior foliar spray for combatting various mildews and rusts and black spot on roses.

But a word of caution here: at all costs, beware of

trendiness in weeds. Horticultural folly is everywhere in these disturbed days, and while a mindless aping of the white garden at Sissinghurst is harmless enough, succumbing to a weed fad can be lethal. Along our newly laid flagstone steps and pathways, a little native wild strawberry was quick to colonize. It looked a bit scrappy to me, but an article in a tony magazine advised that wild strawberries were *the* trendy new groundcover of the day and worth a small fortune at the proper garden shops. Well, say no more, we let our group grow where it would. And, yes, to step outdoors on a June morning and pluck one of the tiny, sweet fruits is a lovely treat. But, as we soon discovered, strawberry runners could sweep the summer Olympics without working up a sweat. They can long jump, high jump, hurdle, and sprint across pathways, steps, and walls in world-class time. Within two years our once-elegant stonework was entirely infested with the little creepers. They get their toenails under the stones and simply will not let go. The moral of this story: eternal vigilance and unceasing distrust of trendiness.

Seasoned gardeners are instinctively suspicious of plants that grow too easily. If nothing's wrong with a plant, something must be wrong. A stout, robust, well-rooted specimen may have a certain rustic charm, but would it stand a chance at the Chelsea Flower Show? The ideal ornamental, we've come to appreciate, should resemble the Victorian ideal of young womanhood—frail, fragile, given to fainting spells, and altogether rather helpless. In such a regime, weeding might appear to be the systematic elimination of plants well suited to a site in order that ill-suited exotics might languish there a little longer.

But certain robust plants, whether natives or exotics, have a claim to land and resources that even the General Custers among horticulturalists must sooner or later acknowledge as legitimate. I don't mean just the native wildflowers that are disappearing from our woodlands, deserts, and grasslands at such an alarming rate. I include as well the more common, weedy characters—the mulleins, yarrows, tansies, and their pals, the tramps who thrive along our roadsides and in our meadowlands. They are inescapably common, and even having them move into the neighbourhood rather tests some people's liberal sympathies.

Unless, of course, a celebrity gardener, preferably someone speaking in an Oxford accent, declares the species to be "in." Then all the class barriers come tumbling down; the security people are advised to let these scruffy strangers through; and an egalitarian bonhomie suffuses the entire estate. Such is the case of the mullein, that Eliza Doolittle of weeds. A commoner through much of Europe and Asia, its thick upright stems were traditionally soaked in tallow to fashion ceremonial torches, earning for the plant two of its nicknames, witches' torch and Our Lady's candle. Also called Our Lady's flannel, for its thick and soft foliage, the great mullein had an established reputation for confounding a witch's hex and warding off evil spirits.

Introduced from Europe, this rough-and-tumble bi-
ennial has colonized many areas of North America,
doing particularly well in dry meadowlands. A familiar
sight along roadsides, it's looked down upon as a common and even noxious weed, especially in cattle country
where its fuzzy foliage discourages browsing. I remember encountering mulleins massed in unruly magnificence while hiking down a mountainside in dry grass-
land range country. Hundreds of the tall flowering stalks
backlit by the westering sun created a remarkable landscape illuminated as by living candles.

As Henry Mitchell puts it, "mulleins are among
those glorious plants that are almost but not altogether
weeds." They are cultivated, he says, "for beauty and
drama, which are by no means the same as a floral riot."
Disciples of Gertrude Jeckyll cherish them. Louise Beebe
Wilder does too. For though it is considered a trouble-
some weed, she writes, it is well suited to either formal
or natural plantings, providing a strong fine line and
remaining picturesque throughout the summer. Penelope
Hobhouse and other authorities write with equal enthusiasm about this commoner.

Reassured by these letters of reference, at our place
we encourage self-seeding witches' candles in the mixed
borders, along the rose arbours and in other spots. The
real wildling *(Verbascum thapsus)* is welcome in moderation, with its green-grey foliage and small, bright,
sulphur-yellow flowers spotted along the two-metre-
high flowering stalk. Even more dramatic, though not
quite so adept a self-sower, is a cultivar—'Gains-

borough'—with silvery-grey foliage and abundant, light
lemon-yellow flowers. This beauty often branches like
an enormous candelabra, lifting its long-blooming candles nearly three metres into the air.

There are other of the so-called weeds we wouldn't be
without. Chickweed springs to mind. Although glamor-
ously named *(Stellaria media)*, this cosmopolitan weed
is problematic for gardeners across the continent for its
persistence in popping up on bare ground. Left alone, its
slender stems and light green foliage form a tatty-looking
mat with tiny white flowers and multiple seed heads.
There are few plants I would rather have than this little
interloper, because it provides us with a ready source of
tender and delicious fresh greens from autumn until
spring. Surprisingly hardy despite its frail appearance, it
collapses in a hard frost but resumes growing the instant
the temperature gets up a bit above freezing. Even in a
severe winter on the coast, it will be putting out fresh
shoots by February. Healthy and tasty, and unusually
rich in copper content, chickweed too has been prized for
centuries as a culinary and medicinal herb. There is no
finer wild salad green; it has the best qualities of water
cress and the tenderest leaves of early spring spinach.
The limp-leafed lettuce offerings of the most exclusive
restaurants are bland mediocrities, laughable rabbit food,
compared with a freshly picked chickweed salad.

Other commoners crowd in to equally fine effect—
miner's lettuce and wild bleeding hearts, rudbeckias, ox-
eye daisies and stinging nettles, street-smart mallows
and foxgloves, yarrows, and tansies and sweet-scented

nicotianas. We welcome them all, as though we're soft-headed aristocrats who've dabbled too much in social-ism. Michael Pollan calls weeds "nature's ambulance chasers, carpetbaggers and confidence men," but I must disagree. Sure there are some rough customers among them, some liars and cheats and shysters who'll make you rue the day you ever showed them generosity. But for every one of these, there's a dozen lovely, charming, helpful characters that you can't banish completely without diminishing both your garden and yourself. Of course they may grow a trifle unruly at times, and perhaps be insufficiently grateful for your forbearance and benevolence. But have you ever pondered Emerson's reflection that a weed is simply a plant whose virtues haven't been discovered yet? I say, is your back giving you trouble?

12

Compost

In their zeal to obtain organic materials for soil improvement, certain gardeners show no shame at all. Point out a couple of cow pies in a pasture or a knot of horse droppings along a bridle path, and they'll start rummaging in their pockets for a bag. A trip to the seashore in their company may soon be ruined by unruly impulses to gather seaweed. Where they can get away with it, they'll enthusiastically trundle all manner of excrement and rotting offal into their back yards. Clandestine deliveries are not out of the question. To these choreographers of decomposition, there's no slop, swill, or sullage, no spilth or filth beneath consideration.

I grew up in a household where this sort of behaviour was commonplace. Saturdays were the worst. That was the day on which my father sometimes visited a nearby sewage treatment plant, returning home in triumph with his '55 Chev awash with buckets of sewage sludge. While the rest of us distanced ourselves as far as possible from the event, he'd dump the sludge into his compost pit, as pleased with himself as though he'd just won a lottery. The stench of the stuff suffused the car and suffused us too when, on the following morning, we drove to church for Sunday mass and had it waft behind us as we walked down the aisle of the crowded church. This malodorous ordeal was too much even for my mother, a magnificent stoic who generally supported the family's commitment to soil improvement at any cost.

So it was with a disconcerting sense of déjà vu that I found myself, twenty years later, engaged in similar undertakings. Determined to improve the tilth in our newly broken garden soils, we scrounged the country-side for anything that would rot. The refined noses with which we'd sniffed our way out of home and through college suddenly became less particular. We spent hours tracking back and forth through the forest behind our place to where the woods give way to pastureland, scooping up sacks of cow manure and packing it home with an absurd sense of accomplishment. The piling up of manure, like the piling up of money, can be an obsessive and intoxicating business. It's said that in Switzerland, of all places, a farmer's wealth was once measured by the size of his manure pile.

We even stooped to murder. Several old-timers put it out that a surefire way to grow whopping crops of tomatoes and cabbages is to bury a large starfish under each plant. Down to the beach we sped in spring, and out onto the tidal flats at low tide. We pried hundreds of purple- and coral-coloured starfish off the rocks they clung to, cast them into potato sacks, dragged them home, and buried them alive beneath our transplants. (All of this predated the emergence of the animal rights movement, and I mention it now in the spirit of a recovered alcoholic recounting past lapses to an A.A. meeting.) The growth results were at best inconclusive. It never occurred to us at the time that the characters proclaiming the merits of buried starfish were also oyster farmers anxious to rid their beaches of starfish because they prey on oysters. The miscalculation of one time leaving a pile of dead starfish too long unattended in the garden resulted in a stench so vile it cured us forever of this questionable starfish slaughter.

But that didn't mean throwing in the towel—like many a fellow gardener hungry for humus, we've cleaned out horse stables, trucked in mushroom manure, bucketed in soybean whey from a tofu shop, happily accepted organic restaurant wastes, and rejoiced in the arrival of several thousand rotting salmon carcasses. All this in the name of soil improvement. Feed the soil, not the plant, urges the old organic adage; there is no wiser path in life than the path of wholesome soil improvement.

Green manuring is a traditional and entirely wholesome approach to soil improvement. Conditioning and fertilizing fields by cover cropping feels as ancient as agriculture itself. In the mild winter climes of the Pacific Northwest, conditions are ideal for winter cover crops. We dig over any bare ground in autumn and plant it thickly with winter rye and vetch. These rugged customers will germinate in the most miserable conditions, grow rapidly, halt during freeze-up and resume growing the instant the temperature rises again. They work authenticated miracles, spreading a labyrinthine root system which prevents precious nutrients from leaching away in winter rains; nodules on the roots fix atmospheric nitrogen in the soil and their biomass adds an enormous amount of organic matter to the soil when tilled in at springtime.

One could be unequivocally enthusiastic about cover cropping were it not for the crops' tendency to superabound. It seems to be a rule of green manuring that by the time you get around to digging it under, the crop is so big it can't be successfully dug. Thick stems resist being chopped up by spade, and the network of nodular roots has coarsened to a hairy mat that grabs the spade and won't let go. I once made the mistake of abandoning my preferred spading, instead bringing in a rototiller to chop the rough stuff in. But the noisy machine's spinning tines were no match for the long stalks of rye. The rototiller bucked and plunged and thrashed around, but was soon bound up uselessly in grass. Time, of course, is of the essence. You're supposed to have the chopping-in completed about a month before planting, allowing the green manure time to rot down. I've found that a day or two before is a more realistic deadline. You also have to get every last scrap of greenery buried, or the stuff will continue growing and quickly overrun your seedlings.

Some authorities refer to green manuring as "sheet composting," but there's another soil-enhancement technique which also goes by that name. This is where people, rather than going to all the time and effort of building a compost pile, simply spread their kitchen scraps, weeds, and other biodegradable rubbish all over the garden with the intention of someday tilling them in. If for any reason the person assigned to tillage falls behind in their duties, an expanse of sheet compost can look uncannily like a sanitary landfill. It's important, when in conversation with people employing this technique, to avoid commenting on the large flocks of gulls and crows scavenging in their yards.

Classical or true composting, on the other hand, has been raised to a level of near mystical significance. British agronomist Sir Albert Howard is widely acclaimed as the founding father of contemporary composting. He vigorously promoted what is called the Indore method of compost making, the conversion of raw organic matter into humus by a series of fermentations. Sir Albert's system works like this: a heap is constructed of successive layers of green matter, manure, and earth, interspersed with sprinklings of ground limestone and rock phosphate. Optimally, a heap should be between two and three metres wide and at least 1.5 metres high and of any length desired. Turned after six weeks and again after a further six weeks, the pile metamorphoses, as though by magic, into dark, rich, crumbly compost.

From its modest beginnings in nineteenth-century colonial India where Sir Albert worked, the compost heap has leapt into contemporary horticulture with the force of a Bengal tiger. Today we're talking power compost, which means we're talking aerobic acceleration. The decomposer organisms that are the workhorses of a compost heap need oxygen, and refreshing their oxygen supply is a principal reason for turning the heap. Certain clever minds soon set to work to find less strenuous ways of getting oxygen in where it's needed. Pipes or stakes penetrating the heap and later pulled out are a primitive way of increasing air supply to the rapidly heating core. Employing mesh retaining walls was found to help too. Then somebody came up with the "open hearth" system, in which the entire pile is built on an elevated grate thirty centimetres off the ground, allowing air to be constantly pulled up through the pile. Hotheads claimed that this system could reduce compost completion time from several months down to six days. Wow!

Then the race was really on. Another inventive spirit figured it was possible to get additional oxygen into the heap by hooking up an old vacuum cleaner and blowing air through it. One deservedly anonymous enthusiast began advocating turning the heap every three or four days, even though this would leave very little time in life for anything else. Some competitors realized that you could speed things up after initial fermentation by sock-ing the heap full of worms purchased for the purpose. Or you could sprinkle in a compost accelerator whose nutrients and enzymes would kick the heap into overdrive. A frenzied competitiveness seemed to seize certain compost makers, and the gentle art threatened to degenerate into something resembling a dogsled race.

The pace really picked up when compost makers realized that by grinding the raw materials you could greatly increase their surface area and radically accelerate decomposition. Grinders and shredders roared into the marketplace. This technological breakthrough in turn ignited an unprecedented entrepreneurial interest in composting. Various mounted bins and tumblers were invented, patented, and marketed. The idea here is that you can just fire in your kitchen scraps and garden debris and give the tumbler a spin every few days in order to aerate and break up the clumps. No fuss, no mess, and high-quality compost in less than a month. Squat polyethylene composting units pushed their way in too, with a promise that the rubbish thrown into the chamber at the top will emerge from the bottom as fresh-smelling, crumbly, black compost. The technological fix was on.

Turning bullish about compost, the market positively boomed with new accoutrements. It became unacceptable in certain circles, for example, to fork one's compost with a standard garden fork, much less a manure fork. You might as soon, while dining, prong your potatoes with your fish fork. Instead, composting etiquette required employing a Scottish composting fork, a lightweight instrument which, claims one catalogue, "appreciably reduces fatigue when turning compost." (Old money, we're led to believe, is still turning compost by hand, bless its tweedy conservatism.) The discriminating shopper can also purchase a stainless steel compost thermometer to surgically penetrate into the middle of a pile and ascertain interior temperatures. Should the heap need a tad more oxygen, you've got your long-handled compost aerating tool designed to probe the heap and stir things up, then easily withdraw. Oh, if Sir Albert could only see us now!

Behind all the hype and flashy paraphernalia, the exotic additives and peculiar rituals, compost makers know that success depends largely upon content. You need the right stuff. And, it goes without saying, the right carbon-to-nitrogen ratio. Thus, as any gardener will attest, a steady supply of fresh manure is worth more than all the fancy tools and tumblers put together. For about a dozen years here we kept both goats and chickens, and lived in composting heaven. Their commingled straw bedding and droppings gave a perpetual supply of topnotch materials, enough for several compost heaps working away all times of the year. Here was wealth beyond measure, but it slipped through our fingers. Bloodthirsty mink, attacking at night, killed so many chickens we gave up, and eventually we got out of goats as well.

Our golden age of compost gone, we now stand alongside countless other gardeners who can only fantasize about mounds of fresh manure. Besides kitchen scraps and garden refuse, our mainstay nowadays is seaweed. As autumn storms begin to blow, we mount a daily watch on the shoreline where our little ferry berths. When conditions are right, the ebbing tide will leave behind a thick litter of sea lettuce, rockweed, and kelp. Islanders scramble to claim this treasure before the returning tide can carry it away.

There are few seasonal chores more exhilarating than this one. Autumn winds whip up the Sound and set the rigging of moored boats singing. The Beaufort Range mountains of Vancouver Island glisten with a fresh dusting of snow, so that even the clearcuts look good. Gulls and cormorants cry. Small waves slap the beach and the intoxicating scent of brine hints of faraway places. As you rake the glistening seaweed into buckets, you feel moved to sing a sea shanty, if only you knew the words. You make a great to-do about "getting in the seaweed," to impress any tourists lined up to catch the ferry. In a mad moment you find yourself doing hearty imitations of old Prince Edward Islanders gathering Irish moss, leaving the departing tourists with Lord knows what illusions about the quaintness of "island life."

Back at home we unload the seaweed and gather whatever else is available. With luck there'll be a last cutting of comfrey leaves; we grow lots of comfrey in wild spots and whack down their fuzzy green foliage with a machete to use as compost activator. Stinging nettles play the same role in the spring. There's always a huge pile of refuse from the garden—uprooted annuals, perennial clippings, and seedless weeds. We don't grind or shred any of this stuff, but in the depths of the toolshed there lurks an ancient lawnmower which I have every intention of someday mounting over a bin to make a grinder/shredder. This intention has stood the test of time remarkably well.

With all ingredients save one at hand, the moment of truth arrives: time to open up the compost privy. This is not an occasion for delicate sensibilities. It is the flip side of the hearty, wind-blown freshness of the beach, a cottage industry variation on my father's sorties to the sewage plant. Our privy sits rather grandly atop a sealed concrete chamber with sloping floor. It is a two-seater, but only one seat is employed at a time. After each individual use, the user pours in a large cupful of screened soil. When one side is full, we cover it completely with soil and leave it alone for a couple of months, switching over to the other side. Then, on compost-making day, one of us will ceremoniously open a large hatch at the rear of the chamber and set to shovelling out the well-aged mixture.

I'll be honest with you: this is not a dainty affair. There is an undeniable pungency to it that might not be to every taste. But such is the obsessiveness of the confirmed compost maker that even the privy's stenchy stuff has its compensations. Think of the nitrogen, you tell yourself. A bracing sense of environmental right-eousness freshens the shovelling. Feeling downright sanctimonious, one marvels that municipalities can continue pouring raw or barely treated sewage into the nearest available waterway.

Several years ago the director of El Salvador's Institute for Appropriate Technology visited our community. His slide show and talk described the institute's work assisting rural residents to build simple compost privies. These were gratifyingly like our own. He showed us wonderful photographs of beaming *campesinos* standing proudly before their new privies, with potted pelargoniums lining the steps. These privies are making a significant contribution to communal composting programs, reducing effluent contamination of waterways and helping revitalize impoverished farmland in that ravaged country.

Our El Salvadoran guest knew what we too had eventually figured out: that ultimate success depends upon separating urine and faeces. We pee into buckets and pour the accumulated urine over compost heaps as a way of stimulating decomposition, maintaining adequate moisture in the heap, and adding precious urea and other elements to the compost.

Many of us new pioneers who converted to composting privy systems soon discovered that the technology leads to a certain thinning-out of house guests. There are those who simply can't abide the thought of not flushing. I'm the opposite: I'm at the point where I can't stand seeing all those valuable nutrients being carried off to pollute a beach somewhere. I blush when I flush. Long sojourns in the city become intolerable from the squandering of resources, like visits to Las Vegas, and we soon hasten home before too much more is lost.

And so to work: we pile up alternating layers of garden refuse, seaweed, privy production, kitchen scraps, comfrey leaves, and soil. If more green material's needed to generate pathogen-destroying heat, we'll add a few layers of fresh grass clippings, although these are more prized for mulching. Wool clippings are a traditional compost ingredient, and every so often we'll pop in an old wool sock or sweater. Even under optimum conditions, these take over a year to break down, and are often more trouble than they're worth (but how bonny to impale a bit of Harris tweed on your Scottish composting fork!). Polyesters, on the other hand, are impervious to breakdown, and an old polyester sock masquerading as cotton or wool will emerge from the hottest heap unscathed. Sticks, stones, plastic bags, and beer caps are also regularly unearthed, and mentally laying blame for their presence on everyone but yourself can help fill in the long hours spent turning the heap.

Other substances are *verboten*, and you almost need a Ph.D. in chemistry to keep up with what is or is not currently done. Nutshells, for example, are considered excellent, with the sole exception of walnuts, which emit a chemical that is toxic to bacteria. Fresh wood ashes are similarly toxic. Old Sir Albert recommended successive sprinklings of ground limestone to counteract certain acids formed in the decomposition process, because acidity curtails bacterial activity. Nowadays, however, we're advised not to apply lime because it triggers the release of ammonia which reduces the nitrogen content of the compost.

If so inclined, one can get into tremendously esoteric discussions about what is or is not organic compost material. Cottonseed has lost favour because of pesticide residues, cotton being one of the most pesticide-intensive crops grown anywhere. Organic growers have had an ongoing fracas about superphosphate. Rock phosphate that has been doused with sulphuric acid, superphosphate is obviously not natural, arguably not organic, but unarguably beneficial in a compost heap. A gathering of organic growers hashing out a topic like this is a wonder to behold. Although largely sympathetic to the organic point of view, I personally drew a line in the organic sand over the issue of fish-farm salmon. These are not considered a certifiably organic substance either, due to the synthetic foods laced with antibiotics that penned fish are fed. But when a local fish farmer offered us several tonnes of them, delivered to the door, for free, we swallowed our pseudo-organic scruples and grabbed our fish forks, proving once again that most compost makers have their price.

I find the actual construction of a heap to be wonderfully invigorating work. There's a sweaty muscularity to all that forking and pitching, and the physical rhythm of it excites and stimulates. Like stacking up firewood for winter, it appeals to the hoarder hidden within. I enjoy the brainlessness of the project; it's not like some do-it-yourself carpentry or plumbing assignments where you're having to carefully measure and consider and anticipate three steps ahead. Compost making requires, at most, about six brain cells. The rest of one's mental apparatus is free to wander where it will, to dream and speculate and tapdance across the space-time continuum. One's senses can luxuriate in sun and wind, in the rich aromas rising from the heap and the impertinences of songbirds perched in nearby bushes. For all you know, you might be back among your peasant forebears, straining muscles in the timeless tasks of agriculture. Brimming with endorphins and metaphysical insights, it's almost with regret that you cover the heap with a final blanket of soil and a black plastic sheet and leave it to its mysterious workings.

A few days of careful observation ensue, tinged perhaps with misgivings. Is it starting to heat up yet? I wonder if it's a bit too wet; or maybe not damp enough. Perhaps the weather's too cold for it to get started. I wonder if my carbon/nitrogen ratio was everything it might have been. After several days you find yourself placing your hand on top of the heap trying to detect heat. The plastic's warm all right, but that could be the sun's work, because once again you've ignored repeated advice to build your heap in semi-shade, so the sun won't kill bacteria near the surface. You now seriously consider running to a garden centre to purchase a previously laughable compost thermometer. You realize that you should have been paying stricter attention to what you were doing, instead of all that philosophical tapdancing nonsense.

But within another day or two, a shimmer of heat rises from the heap. You dash out to be sure, and, yes, it's

warm to the touch, wonderfully warm, and working!
Foolishly, you caress it, for there are few creations more
gratifying than a compost heap in heat. It surpasses the
delight of a perfectly risen soufflé or wickedly accurate
graffiti. You rejoice in it, however briefly. Sooner or later
follows the collapse. The heap falls flat, loses its heat,
refuses to go further. You let it be for a bit. But like old
flames, compost heaps, once having cooled, seldom grow
warm again. It's over. You admit to yourself that you'll
have to turn the whole thing soon. Eventually you do,
discovering as you go how much twine, wire, and defi-
antly fibrous plant material you've included, all of which
binds the heap together and prevents its being turned.
This is one of the season's finest opportunities for putting
your back out. Halfway through, pouring sweat, you vow
once again that you'll get that shredder up and running
any day now. Plastic bags, polyester socks, and other
impurities are removed at this stage.

As the revived mound rises anew, you feel again the
stirrings of that old infatuation. But now the feelings are
deeper and more mature, because the first fruits of
decomposition are already in evidence. Encouragingly, a
host of decomposer allies are in attendance: congrega-
tions of bright pink earthworms wriggle in the best-
rotted pockets; colonies of sowbugs croodle in quiet
corners; beetles and centipedes and many-legged milli-
pedes, like tiny Chinese dragons, dash for cover when
disturbed. You salute them all, co-workers in the industrial complex of compost. And the heap, restacked and
revived, begins its second fermentation.

Twice-turned, the heap approaches a moment for critical evaluation: is it done? Ideal compost is the stuff you see pictured in the catalogues spewing from those tumbling drums: photogenically rich, dark, and crumbly. It looks good enough to use as hamburger substitute. Your product, by comparison, is undeniably fibrous. At best it's what the manuals call "partially decomposed." You could turn the heap yet again and bring it tantalizingly close to perfection. But does time permit? Demand outstrips supply, always. No gardener, no matter how big the pile, has enough compost. Supply-side limitations can raise prickly questions about allocation. When orchard, flower gardens, and vegetable patch all cry out with equal voice, how to decide? Some gardeners respond with a frugality, almost a stinginess of spirit, when dishing out compost. If compost is black gold, then these pinched souls are its misers. But who can blame them? The heap that seemed so enormous at turning-time has somehow shrunk by distribution day to little more than a few handfuls. Time, you realize, to get another heap under way.

A year ago we threw all caution to the winds and ordered a dumptruckload of commercial compost, a full twenty yards. Composed of wood chips and dead salmon, the stuff was fabulously dark and rich. Dumped near the driveway, the new heap loomed like Everest above our little homemade heaps. Twenty yards of compost, what luxury! We piled it on wherever it was needed, and in no time at all it was gone. Gone completely, just like all the rest.

There is no honourable escape from compost making, nor should there be. The heap is the garden's hub, its axis of decay and transformation. The alchemy that takes place here is part your doing, part nature's. She supplies raw materials and a willing workforce—a million or more micro-organisms swarming in a teaspoon of compost—while you add managerial expertise. You consolidate nature's workings, give them compaction and pithiness. From her sprawling epic of decomposition, you compose taut short stories.

Leaning philosophically upon your compost fork, you reflect for a moment upon the beauty of the process, its fusion of earthiness and ecstasy, its collaboration of natural and human genius, its eternal enthusiasm for transformation. This, you tell yourself, is recycling and reusing at its most sublime. You wax enthusiastic, and detect herein a paradigm for the planet as a whole: if only everyone could keep a compost heap, the world would be...

13

Wildlife

There's a lot of emphasis nowadays on ecological gardening as a means of creating habitat to attract backyard wildlife. I'm all for it. Still, as any reputable wildlife biologist will tell you, the introduction or reintroduction of creatures often brings its own peculiar set of problems. The first requirement of the wildlife gardener is to decide what ought to be drawn in and what kept out. If the neighbour's Saint Bernard deposits a monumental pile of excrement on your lawn every morning, should this be viewed as success in attracting fauna? Probably not. Recently I listened to a heart-breaking story narrated by a woman caller on a local radio gardening phone-in show. She was at the end of her tether over defecating dogs. She claimed that they came from miles around just to squat on her place. Things had been brought to a head by a fresh fall of snow against which the dogs' droppings were brilliantly visible for all to behold. She was no longer sure that she could cope. Suitably empathetic, the talk-show host recommended the planting of prickly bearberries to repel the dogs, but I'm not sure the caller was convinced. We sensed a tone of weary resignation as she hung up.

This sort of situation could drive a person mad, but that's not necessarily a bad thing: at our place I find that free-roaming dogs respond rather well to insanity in homo sapiens. Spotting an intruder, I charge after it, screaming and flapping my arms like a deranged stork, scooping up stones and hurling them. I advocate abandoning all inhibition in this exercise. Males particularly can use the opportunity to get in touch with their wild man within. I've not tried the technique on a pit bull yet, and may not, but I take considerable pride in having once routed a pair of big Dobermans with my raving lunatic charge.

Cats need a firm hand too. We all know that cats love a bit of freshly turned earth, preferably planted, which they can excavate for their toiletries. Usually this occurs under cover of darkness, and when you do catch a cat in the garden, it stares back insolently, as though it were a hoodlum punk defying you to prove that it committed the crime. Don't be fooled by this: all cats are guilty of something. I find that with most feline trespassers the mad dog charge is not an appropriate response. For one thing, most cats have doting owners who are invariably looking out a window at you just as the battle is joined. Instead, a cold catward stare, a malevolent sotto voce hissing and a slow but menacing advance, peppered with subtly flung pebbles, does the trick while maintaining necessary decorum.

Dogs and cats may be the commonest culprits, but veteran gardeners stay alert for all manner of strange invasions. Just recently, Sandy's sister Barbara spotted a large black bear taking apart her compost heap. Valuing compost more than life itself, as any true gardener would, Barbara charged out of the house and, somewhat impetuously, turned the garden hose on the intruding bruin.

Or there's the melancholy story of Hornby Island, just across the water from us, where some genius not long ago introduced opossums. These characters are not native to the islands, but they know a good thing when they see one. With litter sizes up to eighteen, abundant supplies of food, and no predators to control them, the marsupials quickly multiplied to the level of menace, raiding chicken houses and gardens and wreaking havoc on grape vines, fruit trees, and garbage cans. Residents flapped and fumed, issued threats, and set traps. One Hornby Islander with a badly warped sense of humour secretly planted a possum corpse alongside a Denman roadway, thinking to panic us into believing the plague had reached our shores as well. Needless to say, local stalwarts weren't taken in by this tomfoolery.

I remember other invasions. One morning, years ago, after a thumping great storm, we scooted down to the beach and loaded the truck with a grand haul of seaweed. Back home, we stacked it in a heap near the garden, intending to spread it as mulch on the vegetables. In those days we were living in a dirt-floor log cabin near the garden. That evening we found the place being invaded by weird little hopping creatures. We were accustomed to all sorts of unusual intrusions—snakes, frogs, and slugs often passed through—but what the hell were these things? I went out to investigate. There were thousands of them, hopping methodically from the seaweed heap towards our cabin. Of course, sand fleas! They were being drawn by our lights. We dimmed the kerosene lamps, and the fleas hopped back to their seaweed, where they remained active for several days before meeting what can only have been a gruesome end.

Tent caterpillars are another strand in the great web of life that can leave the gardener unstrung. We used to have grotesque infestations of them in young alder trees. There's something inordinately menacing about these big sticky tents wriggling with hundreds of black caterpillars, like maggots in carrion. I once encountered an infestation of them in a copse of big poplar trees where their collective munching was so loud it could be heard from the ground, ten metres below them. I tried spraying the tents in our fruit trees with insecticidal soap, to not very great effect. In a "hands-on" phase, I scooped the tenty messes out of the trees and methodically ground the whole squiggling mass under my boot heel. Yech!

Then somebody put me on to the scorched earth approach. This involves firing up a butane cylinder with a mini-flamethrower nozzle and torching the poor caterpillars in their tents.

Years have now elapsed since we've had any tent caterpillars. Did my indecent assaults upon them prove an effective deterrent? Not likely. I suspect some helpful bird or other is keeping them in check, and I'm grateful. My only question is this: why don't wild birds eat sowbugs? We have untold thousands of these little characters, which some people call wood bugs or pill bugs. They look like tiny slate-grey armadillos, huddled in conspiratorial groups in damp, dark places. Lift a board or rock anywhere and dozens of them will go running for cover. They love strawberries. Sometimes I'll pick a beautifully ripened large strawberry and, turning it over, find the entire underside has been excavated by sowbugs. Same with bell peppers: they'll tunnel their way inside a pepper, particularly if it's touching the ground, and spend their days happily eating and defecating in this moist, dark chamber almost custom designed for their comfort. Toads are supposed to be excellent for controlling sowbugs, and chickens love them. We have neither; so sowbugs we have by the bucketload.

Sowbugs are only one of the stars in the rogue's gallery of pests gardeners come to know so well. With cutworms and wire worms, leaf rollers and root maggots, aphids and tomato worms all wriggling about, one feels a mighty temptation to classify every squiggling life form as a pest and launch pre-emptive strikes against the lot of them. The dilemma is in knowing what you're dealing with. I'm forever coming across various caterpillars, pupae, larvae, and tiny nests of eggs and I have no idea what they're destined to develop into. They may represent the early stages of some magnificent butterfly that will thrill us with its fluttering beauty. Or they could be the beginnings of a malignant infestation that will blight our gardens and our lives in perpetuity. Other gardeners I talk with are in the same fix. Every neighbourhood needs an entomologist who does house calls.

Wise gardeners at least know now that the "why take any chances? kill 'em all" approach doesn't work. Instead, we select the enlightened path of the ecological gardener. We speak, perhaps a bit sanctimoniously, about the wisdom of employing natural controls, about finding harmonic convergence within the great and dynamic equilibrium of Mother Earth.

Many of us look to birds for help—our so-called "feathered friends." Woodpeckers, for example. These, we're told, are invaluable allies in the war against destructive beetles, carpenter ants, and other pests. Several species of woodpecker flit in and out of the woodlands around our place. The first to introduce itself was the pileated woodpecker, a large bird with an absurdly red plume on its head, the quintessential Woody Woodpecker. One spring morning at dawn we were jolted awake by a frantic banging and shrieking right over our heads. We're being attacked by maniacs! we thought.

And we were, sort of. The little cabin we were living in was heated with a wood stove that had a metal stovepipe. Where it exited the roof, the pipe was double-walled and insulated, known as a Yukon chimney. Presumably for reasons of resonance, the woodpecker selected this chimney for its springtime courtship drumming. It would bang its beak repeatedly on the resonating chimney and then let out an hysterical shriek. The loft where we slept was immediately beneath this performance area. When the amorous woodpecker got an answering cry from the distant woods, it would scuttle around on the roof just over our heads and repeat its drumming and screaming like a demented acid rocker in the attic.

Mercifully this performance was confined to the spring mating season, but it wasn't the only unfortunate encounter in what threatened to become a chilly relationship with the woodpecker family. Next came the yellow bellied sapsucker. Only half as big as a pileated woodpecker, these birds are common across the continent. I first noticed one on the trunk of a rather dyspeptic mountain ash growing near our fruit garden. We'd planted the tree following somebody's expert advice that birds prefer wild fruit to domesticated berries. Plant a mountain ash, we were told, and birds will devour its bright red or orange berries and leave your raspberries alone. The fact that mountain ash berries form several months after raspberries didn't enter these early discussions.

I began noticing a ring of small holes in the tree's bark, and realized that the sapsucker was responsible. I didn't yet know the bird by name: I'm not myself a "birder"—one of those eccentric types in gumboots and binoculars who emerge from underbrush around the edges of swamps to tell you excitedly that they've just spotted a Bohemian waxwing. As far as I was concerned, the bird on our mountain ash was some kind of wood-pecker. "Won't those holes damage the tree?" Sandy asked. "Oh, no!" I answered, "it's feeding on destructive insects under the bark; it'll benefit the tree in the long run." This sort of unsubstantiated rubbish, if said in an authoritative tone, usually carries the day, unless you're talking to a birder.

It turned out our sapsucker wasn't after insects so much as sap. Hence the name. It became a regular visitor. At first when we passed close by, it would flit off to a nearby tree and scold us loudly for the interruption. Eventually, the mountain ash was pockmarked with holes up and down its trunk and was weeping sap. The bird was obviously killing the tree and had grown so brazen it wouldn't even take off when we passed within a couple of metres. It would just hop around the opposite side of the trunk and keep on slurping up sap. I began giving it an avian version of the mad dog charge. It would scoot off into a nearby maple, but always with a laughing cry that rang thick with contempt. Only those who have experienced it can know the emotional scarring that can occur from being jeered at by a yellow-bellied sapsucker.

Soon after our gardens were established the robins moved in. Familiars of gardeners across the continent, these aren't the charming little robin redbreast of Europe, after which they were named by homesick settlers. The fat fellows we call robins are really a species of thrush. But while their near relatives, like Townsend's solitaire and the hermit thrush, retain a mystique of solitary birds glimpsed during wild rambles through woodlands, robins hang around the yard like laundry.

They might be the perfect mascot for gardeners because robins too love to root around in ground. One autumn I made the mistake of planting out scores of small perennials, raised from seed and cuttings, in small pots which I sank into soil and mulched with fine grass clippings for winter protection. By early spring, industrious robins had scraped away all the mulch while hunting for insects (not sowbugs, of course) and in the process uprooted or smothered many of the little plants. Having spent considerable time fussing with seedlings and softwood cuttings the previous summer, to now see most of them scattered dead on the ground and a queue of plump robins sitting on the fence caused a momentary dimming of my commitment to ecological gardening.

Ever the opportunists, robins are perfectly happy if somebody else does the digging for them, and when I get to spading over the vegetable patch they really tuck in. The question here is how close they dare to get in order to swipe an earthworm brought up by the spade. Turn your back for a moment and they're in like pickpockets. This worm work is at its most furious when voracious nestlings are demanding non-stop food. On our grounds, the robins cleverly nest in big cedar trees all around the

garden, thus cutting down the commuting distance between workplace and home. Prior to nest establishment,
fierce battles are fought over territorial rights to the easy
pickings in our garden.

To the victors go the worms—and the berries. Robins
have an uncanny knack for producing a brood that will
fledge just as strawberries or raspberries ripen. As the
first pale hints of pink begin to blush across the berries,
what had been a handful of diligent parent birds suddenly
multiplies into a host of hungry fledglings. Now the
fundamental absurdity of the "birds prefer wild berries"
hypothesis lies fully exposed. Our place is all but overrun
with wild berries—huckleberries, thimbleberries,
salmonberries, blackberries, elderberries, wild strawberries, raspberries, and gooseberries. It's a jungle out there,
a wildlife gardener's fantasy made flesh. But where do the
robins congregate? Half of them are busy getting trapped
under the nets I laboriously spread to keep them off the
strawberries. The other half are working over the raspberry canes. You walk into the garden and clouds of birds
explode out of the berry patch, like clay pigeons at a
shoot.

Under this kind of provocation, a person might be
tempted to launch retaliations. But the foolish way of
war is not the way of the wildlife gardener. One bides
one's time, knowing full well that what goes around
comes around. Sure enough, the robins, secure in what
looks like a permanent free lunch in the berry patch, set
about producing a second brood. Then the wildlife gardener, like a magician pulling doves from a top hat,

unveils the pièce de résistance: great horned owls.

A pair of these big beauties nests every spring in the woods near our house. At night their preternatural cries echo through the darkened forest, haunting calls from the nether world. After nesting season, they perch on low tree branches around our clearing in broad daylight, enormous and profoundly wise-looking. Here's the fun part: they drive the robins crazy. You can tell right away when there's an owl nearby from the furious, high-pitched shrieking of the robins. Groups of robins, probably seeing the owl as a threat to their offspring, surround the intruder and scream bloody murder. They'll dive-bomb it, and particularly reckless robins will fly at a perched owl, striking it a glancing blow in passing. To the harassed wildlife gardener, the robins' hysteria is sweet revenge for their pilferings. But, as always, it soon sours. The owls hang around for weeks, and the robins keep screeching at them. Hour after hour, day after day. Pretty soon you're ready to scream too, and call down a pox on all these "feathered friends."

***

The telephone bird may be the worst of all. This is a woodland dweller whose call consists of a clear single note repeated at intervals and completely indistinguishable from the ringing of a telephone. Some gardeners, I know, pack a portable telephone around with them in the garden; others have installed outdoor bells which, when the phone rings indoors, send a piercing ring reverberating through the neighbourhood. But most gardeners, like myself, are instead trained in the discipline of the telephone dash.

We're expecting an important call, but we also need to get a few things done in the garden. We leave windows and doors open so that we can hear the phone ring. When we're at the point in the garden farthest from the phone, it rings. Or at least we think it rings. We straighten up and listen. Was that the phone? we ask. Uncertain, we strike one of the classic poses of the seasoned gardener: ear cocked, listening for the phone, like an attentive grouse at mating season. If it rings again, we explode into motion with the splendid acceleration of a track star. Leaping heaps of intervening vegetation without breaking stride, a high hurdler in full flight, we traverse garden, steps, patio in seconds and arrive at the shrilling phone just as it stops ringing. On the odd occasion when we get there in time, the call will be from somebody wanting to shampoo our rugs or sell us a side of freezer beef.

The telephone dash is a nuisance, but most of us accept it, as we accept powdery mildew, as a necessary component of gardening life. The telephone bird, however, carries things one step too far. Its shrill cry, so uncannily like a telephone ring, throws all into confusion.

Was that the phone?
I don't know.
Yes, that's the phone.
No, I think it's the bird.
That's not the bird, it's the phone.
Maybe you're right.

Then off I go, dashing haplessly. Precious seconds have

been squandered in indecision and, with them, all hope of getting to the phone in time.

The ecological gardener is a Machiavellian master, ever alert for opportunities to forge alliances with fellow creatures against common adversaries. With the slick felicity of a foreign diplomat, the gardener encourages and cajoles potential allies, rewards and flatters those who can be of use. None is cultivated more assiduously than the ladybug. Named "Our Lady's Bird" for its close connection with the Virgin Mary, the ladybird has since ancient times been considered magical, and was intimately associated with Isis, the Egyptian goddess of magic. Tiny as it may be, the ladybug carries more legends, myths, and rituals about itself than do many creatures ten thousand times its size.

So the gardener may be forgiven an excess of enthusiasm about ladybugs. They're especially renowned as aphid predators, and aphids, like sowbugs, are seldom in short supply. The larvae of ladybugs—strange, alligator-shaped creatures—gorge themselves on aphids, and adult ladybugs carry right on devouring aphids along with mites, mealy-bugs, and scale insects. Some pest-plagued gardeners order cartons of ladybugs by mail and scatter them around the garden. This is an act of ecological gardening in the broadest sense, although purists frown upon mail-order fauna. Far preferable, they argue, is the creation of habitat amenable to wild ladybugs who'll then come winging in on their own.

This has proved to be the case at our place, where we've seen a slow but steady increase in populations. Last spring I came upon a whole herd of them milling around on a stinging nettle plant. I suspect that they'd only just emerged as adults. I stood aside and hailed them gratefully as each took wing, like a miniature Billy Bishop, off to do battle in the aphid war. I felt they needed encouragement because we sometimes get aphids so thick they'll totally coat the new green tips of broad beans and the stems of Russian kale.

As aphid colonies expand—they can produce twenty generations in a year—one's faith in unaided ladybugs begins to waver. Then you're stuck with the dilemma: do you spray the aphids with insecticidal soap and risk killing off ladybug larvae that may be busy browsing on the aphids? Spraying might also endanger the eggs and larvae of certain parasitic chalcid wasps. The female wasp oviposits each of her eggs inside a living aphid, and when it hatches, the wasp larva consumes its host aphid from the inside out. This is precisely the sort of thing you want to encourage, and not go wrecking with an ill-timed spray.

And the aphid has its allies too: armies of fierce ants that march around farming and guarding the aphids. In payment for protection, aphids feed the ants a sweet, sticky liquid called honeydew which they secrete from the anus. At our place the redheaded ants that take up with aphids are no laughing matter. They live in colonies that can grow to enormous size. I've encountered ant hills in the bush well over a metre in diameter and stacked up with twigs and conifer needles more than half a metre high. The countless thousands of ants milling around in this megalopolis make enough noise that you can hear the rustling of the hill from several metres away.

Every so often, a new colony gets established or a colony relocates, like tropical army ants marching purposively to a new bivouac. When ants choose a site for their new hill within the ecologically sound garden, they create a real quandary. The well-intentioned authorities who tell you that ants don't cause problems in a garden have never dealt with the fierce legions we have. Once upon a time I used to give misplaced ant colonies a little splash of Diazanon and that was the end of that. Recognizing the error of my ways, I put aside poisons and adopted a program of manual control. I tried flooding, fire-bombing, and excavation of their hills, all to no avail. As a holding action, I've taken to smearing Tanglefoot paste around the trunks of fruit trees, which effectively prevents columns of marching ants from ascending to their most productive aphid ranches. Not long ago, a wise woman advised me that ant colonies respond extraordinarily well to polite persuasion. If properly requested to relocate, she assured me, the colony will usually co-operate in doing so. I'm determined to explore this possibility in the coming months. Meanwhile, I'll be doing my level best to lure in additional wasps and ladybugs.

Improving habitat is the real life's work of the wildlife gardener. While logging companies, land developers, and other agents of progress are busy destroying forests and fields, deserts and wetlands wherever there's a windfall profit to be sniffed, gardeners are under increasing pressure to create small sanctuaries for earth's beleaguered creatures. In Britain, the Royal Society for Nature Conservation estimates that so many country ponds have been drained, filled, or contaminated that today the greater part of the wild frog population is dependent upon garden pools.

I can think of no group better suited to shoulder this burden than gardeners. Can you imagine the politicians taking it on? Or what a botch the Army Corps of Engineers would make of it? Armies of frogs, that's what we need now, bales of turtles, plumps of wildfowl, and exaltations of larks. We need landscapes swarming with life forms, as in mediaeval tapestries and illuminated manuscripts. Long accustomed to touching the earth with dexterity and skill, having an ear attuned to the secrets heard in the hum of wild bees, the gardener is perfectly placed for some hands-on conservation work.

Still, some of what's required goes rather roughly against the gardener's grain. Our idea of a garden is pre-eminently one of a clean, well-ordered place. Its lines are finely drawn, its borders crisp, its segments properly compartmentalized. From the days of our ancestors, the garden has been a contrived environment, an artificial patterning set against the random chaos of an uncertain world. Nowadays, at least in "developed" countries, the burden of the garden may be reversed; it becomes instead a sanctuary of wildness, a haven of the haphazard within a landscape increasingly homogenized and manipulated for human needs alone.

Mother Nature is a blowzy kind of character. She prefers her edges blurred, her territory rough and tumble. Wildlife likes it wild. So the ecological gardener, having previously expended vast sums of time and money getting the estate neat and trim, is now called upon to roughen it up. The new ambition is to create an ecologically rich environment which contains all plant layers, supports abundant larval and adult insect food sources, contains sizable undisturbed pockets, and connects naturally with other nearby habitats. Rock piles are left to accommodate snakes; mud pits attract mud daubers; rotting logs and brush piles are perfect for small mammals and amphibians; woody cover, gravel patches, long grasses, and a plenitude of dead and dying matter all foster a rich and diverse wildlife population.

Choked with brambles, rotting logs, and rock piles, the ecological garden begins to resemble a vacant lot. Long hours spent developing an understory that will provide birds and mammals with an assured supply of fruit, seeds, bugs, bark, and foliage fail to impress the neighbours. In vain the gardener explains that the yellow warbler utilizes a particular vegetation layer for courtship, another for nesting, and still another for feeding; to the untrained eye the yellow-warblerized garden looks suspiciously like a briar patch. You begin to notice a certain lifting of eyebrows as you explain that weedy areas are better wildlife habitats than manicured lawns and that ecological design principles require a revolution in our thinking about gardens. You can't escape the suspicion that the neighbours are discussing you in unflattering terms, that they think you've "let your place go." Though you might be out on the cutting edge of eco-gardening, as far as they're concerned your place is a disgrace.

Unfazed by the neighbours, the eco-gardener is forever installing bat houses and swallow boxes and planting peculiar things to attract butterflies and wild bees. There is a yin and yang to wildlife gardening, a delicate balance between letting things be and helping things become.

You know that your wildlife work is really beginning to pay dividends when creatures start taking over your home. House sparrows demonstrate how they came to be named by constantly flying in through open doorways at our place and then trying vainly to escape through closed south-facing windows. Dragonflies are good at this too. I spend a significant part of my summer balanced between the windowsill and couch trying to catch these ancient companions of dinosaurs and remove them to the great outdoors. We also have a nice little summer colony of bats in the attic and a large part of the attic roof is blobbed with the nests of mud daubers. These terrifying-looking but harmless wasps work hard all summer building their muddy nests, inside of which they lay their eggs. Unhappily, in the artificial environment of the house, their offspring emerge at peculiar times and we're often faced in midwinter with the ethical dilemma of what to do with various wasps crawling around in the house. Just the other day, as I was sitting in my study labouring over these very pages, a movement on the floor caught my eye. There, in the middle of the floor, sat a brilliantly green little tree frog, staring up at the bookcase as though it had dropped in to borrow a novel.

The eco-garden swarms with examples of the perversity of biodiversity. Can the wildlife gardener legitimately entertain ladybugs, snakes, and toads while seeking to exclude squirrels, skunks, and slugs? After great exertion we've developed a nice little pond that now supports a thriving colony of salamanders and red-legged frogs. How are we supposed to react when we see a great blue heron come gliding in like some monstrous pterodactyl and stand at pond edge with its long stiletto beak poised to deliver sudden death to an unsuspecting amphibian? Does one shout and drive it off? Does one stand back and let it all be? Where's the gardener's place in the natural world?

Somewhere, I suppose, in the realms of wonder and delight. At Maytime great swallowtail butterflies come swooping and swirling through our gardens, alighting for a moment as animated petals on poppies and delphiniums. Wild bumblebees disappear down the lovely tunnels of foxglove flowers and re-emerge in reverse, all dusted with pollen, their little saddlebags swollen with nectar. Spiderwebs filigreed with droplets of dew stretch backlit by the rising September sun. Well-fed garter snakes bask in plump contentedness on a sun-warmed stone. Occasionally, two mating dragonflies, locked together in a tumbling, iridescent circlet, will land on my shoulder and copulate like miniature mythic dragons. And there is the perfection of ruby-throated hummingbirds hovering alongside honeysuckle flowers; how they alight on a flat stone in our little waterfall and bathe themselves in the cascade, splashing water with their tiny wings; how in spring they come to pluck the fluffy seed heads from a clematis by the door and fly away with them to line their tiny secret nests.

14

Divine Madness

$\mathcal{M}$ost gardeners, as I started out to say, are nuts. In the erratic world of horticulture, cognitive abnormalities abound. One April morning you'll be bustling along past the greenhouse on some urgent errand or other. A drift of red tulips catches your eye. You forget where you were hurrying to, distracted by the numinous beauty of tulips. You draw closer, fascinated. You stoop and reach to touch the nearest bloom. Fine droplets of dew are beaded on the petals. Your fingertips tremble at the touch of living silk. You peer into the blood-red cup with the reverence of a questing knight who has found the Holy Grail. In its depths, profound blackness is etched and flecked with yellows, as though sunspots were erupting from a dark star. Among sooty black anthers at the bottom of the chalice lie what Wordsworth called "the mysteries that cups of flowers enfold / And all the gorgeous sights which faeries do behold."

Does this sound like a rational perception? Of course not, it's a visionary moment, an instant of rapturous delight and sweet repose. With perfect clarity, the very essence of tulipness, brilliant as illuminated rubies, glows in an epiphany of beauty. Ridiculously, you feel as though some Hollywood Tinkerbell had touched you with her magic wand, splashing stardust over you. Somewhere in the background the Mormon Tabernacle Choir is belting out Handel's "Hallelujah Chorus." You're dazzled, enlightened, suffused with overwhelming joy.

Needless to say, this sort of thing can be quite unnerving for someone who only wanted a nice springtime show of tulips. Mystical visions are best left to enthusiastic undergraduates dabbling in Taoism while trekking through Nepal. But by taking up gardening we have, perhaps unwittingly, perhaps unconsciously, entered an enigmatic region where myth and mysticism, not to mention madness, have their roots in earth that is older than history itself.

The gardener putters along a path of ecstasy. It might be strewn with the debris of yesterday's weeding and cleaning frenzy, and farther along, you may have to pause in order to reposition a bothersome rock or murmur encouragement to a distressed transplant. But it's a path of ecstasy nevertheless. From the Greek *ekstasis*, "to stand outside." Nobody can hang around outside the way a gardener can. We're impossible to keep inside when the mood's upon us. Like mystics and lunatics, gardeners stand outside themselves, ravished by the glory of a world magically transformed.

From the perspective of the helping professions, gardening can be looked upon as a fantastically complicated form of regression therapy. We grope our way back in time, discovering pieces of a puzzle. We recall from our own undergraduate dabblings in comparative religion the paradise myths of ancient cultures. These stories all speak of a "nostalgia for paradise," a yearning to return to that place of beauty, freedom, spontaneity, and innocence from which humankind was banished by a fall from grace. The Elysium of the Greeks, where, in Hesiod's words, "the bounteous earth beareth honey-sweet fruit fresh thrice a year." California before freeways. The Island of the Blest, which was for the Celts an enchanted place "without grief, without sorrow, without death."

These ancient visions of a golden age in which humans were once utterly simple, living at peace with themselves and in harmony with all other living things, might not sound exactly like an afternoon spent weeding your shade garden, but they're close. Nostalgia to create again that blessed place, the lost garden, animates the gardener's craft. With trowels and tattered hats in hand, we take our rightful places in a long procession of plantspeople stretching back into antiquity. Ancient Hebrews pictured the first man, Adam, as a gardener appointed by God to tend the garden of Eden. And for thousands of years before that, the great Earth Goddess in various forms taught the people her secrets of planting, growing, and harvesting. Amid the forbidding deserts and hills, fierce winds and sun of the ancient Near East, paradise gardens were born as pleasure parks, where the privileged could recline in shade, soothed by cooling waters and refreshed with succulent fruits. So the word "paradise" literally means, in old Persian, a walled enclosure, a place set apart from its surroundings and made pleasant through cultivation.

Gardeners have been at it ever since. In the gardens of mediaeval monasteries and courtyards, in cottage gardens, country estates, urban allotments, and inner-city window boxes, gardeners through the ages have been grubbing and digging their way back to paradise. In their calloused hands the garden becomes a fragment of paradise refound, a facsimile of the primordial garden, sanctuary from the brutalities and injustices of a fallen world. Happiness, redemption, paradise—these are the secret promises coded within the clever prose and stunning photographs of coffee-table garden books, alluded to in the seductive descriptions of seed catalogues. You might not have thought so when you planted it, but your little petunia patch is nothing less than a mythic quest for the lost garden, to be whole again, to heal the world.

The gardening life may be full of sweet delights, but gardeners are generally not hedonists. Have you noticed how swingers invariably seem nervous and out of place in a garden? How quickly louts are routed by the sight of old-fashioned folk reaping wholesome harvests? In the same way, psychologists agree, it's extremely difficult to gaze for any length of time at the purity of primroses while nurturing meanspiritedness. The War of the Roses was likely the work of oxymorons.

I don't suggest that gardeners are morally superior to others, far from it. Only that the sins of horticulture are largely the peccadilloes of the pure of heart. Serious gardeners might be guilty of excessive fussiness in the selection of cultivars, but they're usually far too busy to have time for adultery. By and large they don't engage in drunken brawls, unless provoked by herbicide drift or flooding from inconsiderate neighbours. Their lies are ordinarily confined to denying the surreptitious use of chemical boosters. Their furtive taking of Irish cuttings, snipped without permission from plants in other people's gardens or in public parks, hardly qualifies as stealing. Vanity there may be a trace of. False modesty almost certainly. Envy perhaps, but justifiable when you consider the outlandish sums of money those new people down the street are lavishing on their place.

They may wander a fair bit off the beaten path, but that doesn't mean gardeners lack sophistication. Wholesomeness should never be mistaken for naiveté. Certain gardeners take exception to being lumped in with birdwatchers and butterfly collectors as guileless crackpots pathetically out of step with the real world of power and passion. Nothing could be further from the truth. For one thing, gardeners are just about the sexiest people around. There's far more raw sensuality in a fine garden than in any nightclub I've ever been in. A single regal lily has more sex appeal than a whole roomful of overdressed stockbrokers wiggling on the dance floor. The ballyhooed sizzle of Hollywood sex is a tepid tedium compared with the lusty erections of hyacinths or the seductive openings of opium poppies. Poet T.S. Eliot may ponder whether he dares to eat a peach; but the gardener plucks a ripe peach fresh from its tree, feels the fleshy texture of its skin, velvet with delicate hairs, and bites boldly into the succulent fruit. Sweet juices explode in the mouth, gush lusciously across the lips and down the chin in a moment of unbridled sensuality.

As certain wild-eyed characters have pointed out, flowers are the reproductive organs of the plants they grow on. They are among the most elaborate, most provocative sexual displays found anywhere in nature. To walk, hand in hand, with someone you love through a garden makes the sin pits of Soho and Bangkok seem about as titillating as the bathroom exploits of prepubescent boys. Flowers throb and tingle with a thrilling lasciviousness. "O lusty May, with Flora Queen," exults an Elizabethan madrigal, and poet Alice Brown describes how "Dame Peony, red and ripe with bloom / Swells the silk housing of her breast." Make no mistake about it: behind the prim formalities of the flower show, beneath the finicky precision of formal floral arrangements there seethes a lusty sensuousness that would shock the most debauched voluptuary.

Take scent for starters. Nothing is sexier than scent, as the fragrance merchants incessantly remind us in steamy magazine ads featuring eroticized young bodies and chemical sniff strips. Just recently I was excited by one of Chanel's offerings, a cologne for men called Egoiste. "To assume he is uncaring or aloof is to misread him," cautions the ad; in reality the brooding hulk in the picture is a caring chap smelling of "sandalwood sparked with the impertinence of coriander." I'd never really thought of coriander as impertinent, but the makers of Obsession, Volupte, and all the rest surely know whereof they speak. Scent and sex are inextricably linked. A recent Gallup poll revealed that over 70 per cent of respondents rated smell as the most important sexual attractant, far ahead of clothing or hair style. Science has revealed that human eggs and sperm literally sniff each other out before conception. Studies have shown that human eggs secrete a substance that attracts sperm, whose cells have microscopic odour receptors that pick up the scent and guide sperm to egg. In some animals scent is so crucial to reproduction that they cannot copulate if their sense of smell is impaired.

None of this comes as any surprise to people who spend long hours puttering around in their fragrance gardens. Scent, after all, is one of the principal lures plants use to attract bees, butterflies, and other pollinating insects to their flowers. Lusty Elizabethans used to feature fragrant benches in their gardens, places deliberately calculated to stimulate olfactory delight. The ground underfoot might be planted with creeping thyme, chamomile, or other aromatic herbs whose scents would be released when touched. Overhead an arbour would be draped in fragrant jasmine, honeysuckle, and antique roses exuding intoxicating fragrances. On the bench itself perhaps a maiden would sit chastely, enduring the inanities of some rascal like Christopher Marlowe muttering: "And I will make thee beds of roses / And a thousand fragrant posies."

It's this quality of bucolic sensuousness that gardeners are mad for. Sandy and I have spared no effort to replicate it in our own rough fashion. Between the flagstones of the main pathway bisecting our garden we planted half a dozen or more different species of creeping thyme. The idea was that in passing along the path, people would crush the aromatic thymes underfoot, thus releasing their spicy scents. The only problem is people won't step on them. Rather than set foot on the thymes, visitors proceed along the path like schoolgirls playing hopscotch, leaping from one clear patch on the path to another. "Step on the thymes!" we want to shout by way of greeting. Although over a metre wide, the path has been reduced to a narrow goat-track down the centre, hemmed in by twin hedgerows of untrodden thymes.

By late March, tumescent hyacinths begin casting their thick, sweet scent across the still-bare gardens. Almost too much of a good thing, almost cloying, smelling hyacinths is like eating banana splits. They are an olfactory outrage. This seems to be the way of aromatic plantings—either you can't smell them at all, or they drench the air with perfume. While hyacinths aromatize outrageously in all directions, shrinking little violets are far more parsimonious with their perfume. In fact, I can't smell them at all. Sandy will burst out of a doorway on an April morning, throw her arms akimbo, close her eyes, inhale with a glow of rapture and exclaim, "Ah! Smell the violets!" Sniff, sniff, sniff—I still don't smell anything. If I bury my schnozzle deep into a posy of little *odourata* violets, I might pick up a faint whiff of scent, nothing more.

Despite being endowed with a generously proportioned proboscis, I feel myself olfactorily challenged, which is why I like the rock 'em, sock 'em scents of plants like valerian. Once known as St. George's herb, this perennial was employed to treat maladies of the heart and brain, and that's about what it smells like—a powerful but vaguely disconcerting blend of sweetness and strangeness. Rock daphne is another of these no-nonsense scenters. It's no good sticking your nose into its dense clump of foliage, you've got to stand back and wait until an invisible ribbon of sweet fragrance brushes against your soul. Wildly excited by the marvellous fragrance from one little daphne in our rock garden, we multiplied her numbers by layerings and now have babies planted at strategic points all over the garden, so that no matter in which direction the gentle winds of May might blow, they will carry to us wafts of her sweet scent. We've employed the same cover-all-the-angles strategy with a *Philadelphus* 'Belle Etoile' which casts a veil of fragrance through all but the warmest hours of the day. Easily multiplied by softwood cuttings, this shrub throws a balmy perfume redolent with hints of exotic places, as though a warm sea breeze were wafting in from faraway Spice Islands.

In the close, muggy evenings of summer the scented garden is at its most provocative. Honeysuckle and old roses still drip the last of their ethereal sweetness into the night air. Nicotiana and evening scented stocks—both such droopy sad-sacks in sunshine—perk up at twilight and begin exuding overpowering perfumes. Drifts of balm waft in from eucalyptus leaves, old-fashioned sweet peas, and catnip. Enormous lilies, trumpets of love arrayed in the moonlight, pour out musky and voluptuous perfumes. You begin to feel a bit tipsy. A bittersweet nostalgia assails your soul. The night air seems thick with careless languor, charged with erotic desire. The sensualist within you stirs...

Who can say why the sweet fragrances of a garden excite such strong responses in us? A rose might smell as sweet by any other name, but would it smell as sweet if it were not a remembered scent? Is the nostalgic sweetness of a rose no more than a learned response? A study of the various odours that evoked feelings of nostalgia was done using groups of people born between the 1920s and 1970s. For the earlier generations, the smell of roses, violets, honeysuckle, hay, and burning leaves ranked high on the list of nostalgia producers. But the study found a pronounced trend away from these natural odours in the nostalgic scent memories of younger people. For those born in the sixties and seventies, feelings of nostalgia were more frequently aroused by the artificial odours of Windex, scented magic markers, mothballs, and Cocoa Puffs.

Whatever the source, we know that certain scents soothe us. In New York City, high-stress executives skip the traditional relaxing stroll through a garden in favour of a quick aromatherapeutic fix at a centre for holistic medicine. There, for fifty dollars an hour, they can relax and unwind while inhaling the fragrances of jasmine, lemon, and sassafras. A study conducted at a cancer treatment centre in the same city determined that cancer patients undergoing an uncomfortable diagnostic procedure suffered significantly less stress when sniffing the fragrance of heliotrope flowers.

I don't think we gardeners begrudge this fast-food approach to fragrance, but it's not my idea of a good time. Far better to press your cheek softly against a fragrant rose such as 'Maiden's Blush', that sublime alba whose French name ('Cuisse de Nymphe') translates literally to "the thigh of a passionate nymph." I love the smell of tomato foliage on my fingertips after pinching out unwanted shoots and the aromatic essence of pelargoniums that comes from deadheading these bogus geraniums. Not to mention all the other good smells of the garden— the wonderful pungency of fresh-spaded soil in spring; the fustiness of the compost heap; the dewy essence of new-mown grass on a midsummer morning; or the symphony of rich aromas in the garden after a long-awaited September rain. Call me a hopeless romantic if you will, a child of the nature-nostalgic forties, but I'll take these glorious scents every time over the nasal inanity of Cocoa Puffs.

"Oh, it's so peaceful here!" gardeners tell one another, wistfully clinging, against all odds, to the sweet delights found in the sounds of silence. And here I want to give you fair warning: I am a person who has lost all sense of perspective, abandoned the restraints of common decency, around the issue of noise pollution. Noise is now so commonplace—I mean obtrusive, offensive, unnecessary, and overwhelming noise—people need selective hearing to filter out meaningful sounds from the background bedlam, the way clams filter plankton from seawater. Spoiled in the country, when I visit a city it takes me several days to become acclimatized to the thunder and rumble of internal combustion engines, the squeal of brakes and wail of sirens, and all the other components of an unholy polyphony.

But the countryside is far from silent too. The little island I call home is one of those places travel writers love to gush over for its tranquility, its serenity, its peace and quiet. But it's all relative. Certainly compared with the mad din of a major city our small spot is quiet enough, but it's still too noisy by half. People who study sound say that the background hum of traffic can be heard up to sixteen kilometres away. In an otherwise quiet world, the scream of a chain saw carries for about eight kilometres. Even the insidious hum of high-voltage transmission lines reverberates for about three kilometres. A major airport can cast a "noise shadow" eighty kilometres long. At our place we have a reliable source of noise from warplanes stationed at a nearby airbase and low-flying civilian aircraft piloted by scoundrels with smaller brains than the birds they fly among. It's been said that hearing is the sense most intimately connected to our emotional states, and I've personally spent a lot of time shaking a defiant fist and screaming at the top of my lungs at intrusive aircraft disturbing the silence. I picture myself, not long hence, as one of those deranged shouters on inner-city street corners, the true prophets of our age, bellowing the anger and torment of the times back at the implacable roar of autos.

But when the din of highway traffic does at last grow dim—blown perchance in another direction by a heaven-sent wind—when the chain saws and lawnmowers lie silent in their sheds, and all aircraft are miraculously grounded for a moment, when even the neighbourhood dogs neglect their solemn calling to bark unceasingly, then can we enter peacefully the hushed serenity of the garden soundscape. Wind chimes tinkle in the benevolent breeze. A little waterfall splashes and gurgles merrily. Wild bees create a busy humming in the blossoms. A slender garter snake makes crinkling noises as it slithers off across dry leaves. Songbirds splash in a bird bath, and dragonfly wings flutter and click through an aerial tarantella. Pensive in this interlude, you hear the gentle sounds of spent foxglove flowers cascading down their leafy towers to the ground. Quieter still, you detect the tiny raspings of a wasp scratching particles of wood from a fencepost to carry away for nest building. In this golden moment of tranquility, you drift away and float in a reverie of singular delight. The peace that surpasses understanding. Then a lawnmower coughs, sputters, and roars to life nearby. A truck rumbles past. Here comes that confounded jet helicopter again. Down the street the dogs are barking. The wall of sound returns.

Touching and caressing are encouraged within the sensual garden, although some of us behave as though they were forbidden pleasures. The guys, of course, are especially inept. Klutzes, we touch, if at all, roughly, and recoil at the notion of fondling foliage. Keep your hands to yourself, buster, the bellflowers seem to warn, the way Bette Davis would. But some plants cry out to be touched. Take the lovely little lamb's ear. Its woolly grey leaves are delightfully soft, and stooping to caress them gives a tactile thrill quite different from what other senses might excite. The furry new wood of a staghorn sumac reminds you of the touch of velvet on a wild stag's antlers, not that you've ever touched a wild stag's antlers. The leathery leaves of *Viburnum rhytidophyllum*, the palpable perfection of waxen lilies, the military rectitude of spiked yucca leaves, ethereal softness of poppy petals, the feather boa brush of smoke tree flowers—sensuous glories all.

Add in the solid, grainy warmth of sandstone in the sun, the rough bark of Druidic oak trees, paper-thin parchment of birches, the spiny cudgel of a devil's club, swelling tumescence of new rhubarb shoots, the silken smoothness of clematis petals—each of them thrilling to touch. Is anything more profoundly right than the plumpness of a vine-ripened tomato plucked on a warm August afternoon? I like the primitive feel of soil as I grope underground for new potatoes, then find them, fleshy and thin-skinned. Or the tingling cold kiss of dew drops on a cowslip at dawn.

Among the many oddities of gardeners, none mystifies me more than the choice some make to labour long over ornamentals, but never to grow a fruit or vegetable. Ironically these gardens are often described as tasteful, although there's nothing in them to taste at all. Sandy and I live on the other side of the horticultural tracks. The honest pleasure, not to say necessity, of eating what we grow gets top priority in the economy of our place. Our orchard, berry patch, and vegetable garden were established long before we entertained many highfalutin ideas about ornamentals. Even now, if time is pressing or compost in short supply, the needs of the vegetable patch take precedence.

This might seem like bare-knuckle pioneering of the dreariest sort, but in reality vegetable growers know that non-vegetable growers live in a state of deprivation, of gustatory poverty. Relying upon the greengrocer or supermarket for "fresh produce," these poor souls are like ancient mariners nibbling on sea biscuits and slowly succumbing to scurvy. New cookbooks à la Provence won't help them, nor will the haute cuisine at the most recently fashionable eatery. They do not know the simple ecstasy of organically grown corn plucked from the stalk and rushed to the simmering pot, or the rapture of ripe peas popped from pod to mouth without a moment's diminishment of sweetness. Their travel-weary California lettuce wilts beside vibrant green leaves picked ten minutes before lunch, and the glory of fresh garden strawberries has nothing in common with those bland, steroid-boosted bruisers in the shops.

But, let's be frank, some gardeners are going overboard over edibles; for instance, growing vegetables mixed in with ornamentals. Here a plump cabbage squats uncomfortably beside Icelandic poppies. Over there a clump of kohlrabi cluster beneath the bleeding hearts like misplaced Martian spaceships in a gothic romance. Despite having once achieved a brilliant effect with a row of bronzed rhubarb chard and late-season red cabbages planted beneath hanging ropes of amaranth, I'm not really a fan of this commingling. Unabashedly traditionalist on the point, I maintain that vegetables, like small boys, benefit from the discipline of straight rows and a firm hand. Set loose amid the eccentricities of ornamentals, they are apt to lose their heads and grow silly.

Admittedly, the current vogue for edible flowers combines, for a change, prevailing taste and common sense. There's nothing livens up a summer salad like the peppery tang of nasturtium blossoms. Purple violets can ameliorate the unremitting green of spring salads. Pure white *Arabis* blossoms find their way into our spring-time salad bowl too, and it's impossible to keep little Johnny-jump-ups from jumping in. We've taken to tossing borage flowers and rose petals into all sorts of dishes, and the nectar-sweet tips on aquilegia blossoms are a splendid summer treat. But, please, all things in moderation! Knowing the excesses of enthusiasm to which certain gardeners are prone, I can see them carrying this "incredible edibles" fad to extremes, prowling the garden primarily for something to chew on, browsing with the dim single-mindedness of a goat at pasture.

One spring morning you catch sight of a variegated hosta whose new shoots are just now breaking from the earth, bristling like the gathered pennants of mediaeval knights. Nearby the amber stalks of peonies glisten in the chill spring air. The first returning hummingbird hovers by a cluster of red currant blossoms. Atop a moss-draped ancient cedar stump, a huckleberry bush is brushed with a smoky haze of tiny pink-green leaves, and over the dark waters of the pond a weeping willow is all delicate yellow-greens. The burnished green and purplish-copper leaves of bergenia shine like rain-stained bronze. Wild bees are humming among the tiny spires of purple-blue grape hyacinth. In a sheltered alcove, a camellia blushes into bloom, soft pink flowers set against waxy green leaves, heartbreakingly demure, as pure as the first soft stirrings of adolescent love.

In the pearly grey light of dawn, you wander through the garden enraptured. The white flowers of dogtooth violets hang like floating stars of morning. Nearby the blue-grey nubs of Solomon's seal unfurl from the earth like the solemn mitres of bishops assembled for prayer. The foliage of bleeding hearts spreads a tracery of Spanish lace. Along the lips of lady's mantle leaves, infinitesimal drops of dew are strung like filigreed silver. Rolled fiddleheads of bracken fern unfurl, and new sword fern fronds rear up, like elongated Chinese dragons, rusty-red at their rampant heads. Looking up, you're startled by the hazy drifts of blue forget-me-nots, the royal blue of bluebells massed beneath white flowering crab apples. Plump robins court on the lawn and five bald eagles float in a widening gyre high above, their shrill cries thrilling.

Now is the moment of the gardener's bliss, of sweet memories and half-remembered longings, of lost innocence and magical landscapes glimpsed long ago, of all the sentimental, silly, splendid dreams you've ever dreamed. Spirit, soul, senses, memory, imagination, all of them coalesce for just a moment. It is birth and death and all the bittersweet beauties that lie between distilled into one timeless instant. You hang suspended, outside yourself, ecstatic. It's why, in the end, I suppose, you're still crazy about gardening.

Recommended Reading

Here's a list of books that I particularly liked for their information and entertainment value.

Bennett, Jennifer. *Lilies of the Hearth*. Camden East, Ont.: Camden House, 1991.

Carleton, R. Milton. *Your Garden Soil—How to Make the Most of It*. Princeton: D. Van Nostrand Co., 1961.

Chatto, Beth. *The Green Tapestry*. London: Harper-Collins, 1991.

Chompton, James. *Success With Unusual Plants*. London: Collins, 1987.

Crowe, Sylvia. *Garden Design*. New York: Hearthside Press Inc., 1959.

Dennis, John V. *The Wildlife Gardener*. New York: Alfred A. Knopf Inc., 1985.

Francis, M. & Hester, R.T., editors. *The Meaning of Gardens*. Cambridge, Mass.: The MIT Press, 1990.

Fukuoka, Masanobu. *The One-Straw Revolution*. Emmaus, Pa.: Rodale Press, 1978.

Harris, Marjorie. *The Canadian Gardener*. Toronto: Random House, 1990.

_____. *Ecological Gardening*. Toronto: Random House, 1991.

Hobhouse, Penelope. *Color In Your Garden*. Boston: Little, Brown & Co., 1985.

Jekyll, Gertrude. *Colour Schemes For The Flower Garden*. Salem, N.H.: The Ayer Co., 1983.

Johnson, Hugh. *The Principles of Gardening*. New York: Simon and Schuster, 1979.

Lima, Patrick. *The Harrowsmith Perennial Garden.* Camden East, Ont.: Camden House, 1987.

Lovejoy, Ann. *The Year in Bloom.* Seattle: Sasquatch Books, 1989.

_____. *The Border in Bloom.* Seattle: Sasquatch Books, 1990.

_____. *American Mixed Borders.* New York: Macmillan, 1993.

McGourty, Frederick. *The Perennial Gardener.* Boston: Houghton Mifflin Co., 1989.

Miles, Bebe. *Bluebells and Bittersweet.* New York: Van Nostrand Reinhold Co., 1969.

Mitchell, Henry. *The Essential Earthman.* New York: Farrar, Straus and Giroux, 1981.

Page, Russell. *The Education of a Gardener.* London: Penguin Books Ltd., 1985.

Perényi, Eleanor. *Green Thoughts.* New York: Random House, 1981.

Pollan, Michael. *Second Nature.* New York: Atlantic Monthly Press, 1991.

Thaxter, Celia. *An Island Garden.* Boston: Houghton Mifflin Co., 1894 (reprinted 1988).

Verey, Rosemary. *The Scented Garden.* New York: Van Nostrand Reinhold Co., 1981.

Wilder, Louise Beebe. *Color In My Garden.* New York: Atlantic Monthly Press, 1918 (reprinted 1990).